ELEMENTARY TEACHER'S HANDBOOK OF

INDOOR AND OUTDOOR GAMES

Art Kamiya

PARKER PUBLISHING COMPANY
West Nyack, New York 10994

Library of Congress Cataloging-in-Publication Data

Kamiya, Arthur.
    Elementary teacher's handbook of indoor & outdoor games.
    ISBN 0-13-260845-6 (pbk.)
      1. Educational games—Handbooks, manuals, etc.
  2. Group games—Handbooks, manuals, etc.   3. Activity
programs in education—Handbooks, manuals, etc.
  I. Title.
LB1029.G3K35   1985   85-9358
371.3'07'8   CIP

Printed in the United States of America

20   19   18   17

ISBN 0-13-260845-6 (PBK)

ATTENTION: CORPORATIONS AND SCHOOLS

Parker Publishing Company books are available at quantity discounts with bulk purchase for educational, business, or sales promotional use. For information, please write to: Prentice Hall Career & Personal Development Special Sales, 240 Frisch Court, Paramus, NJ 07652. Please supply: title of book, ISBN number, quantity, how the book will be used, date needed.

PARKER PUBLISHING COMPANY
West Nyack, NY 10994

A Simon & Schuster Company

On the World Wide Web at http://www.phdirect.com

Prentice-Hall International (UK) Limited, *London*
Prentice-Hall of Australia Pty. Limited, *Sydney*
Prentice-Hall Canada Inc., *Toronto*
Prentice-Hall Hispanoamericana, S.A., *Mexico*
Prentice-Hall of India Private Limited, *New Delhi*
Prentice-Hall of Japan, Inc., *Tokyo*
Simon & Schuster Asia Pte. Ltd., *Singapore*
Editora Prentice-Hall do Brasil, Ltda., *Rio de Janeiro*

ELEMENTARY TEACHER'S HANDBOOK OF INDOOR AND OUTDOOR GAMES

Jeremy   Travis   Hana

Elizabeth Artie

I dedicate this book to my wife and family . . .

About the Author

Art Kamiya is the physical education consultant for the State Department of Public Instruction for the state of North Carolina. Prior to this position, he was an elementary physical education teacher for the Wake County Public Schools in Raleigh, North Carolina.

Mr. Kamiya has written numerous articles in the area of education. He is also the editor of *The Great Activities Newspaper,* an elementary physical education publication for both physical education and classroom teachers.

Mr. Kamiya received his undergraduate degree from California State University at Los Angeles and a masters degree in physical education from the University of North Carolina at Chapel Hill.

About This Book

The purpose of this special resource is to provide additional ideas and activities to help enhance the academic, social, and physical needs of the elementary school student. Designed for use by both the classroom teacher and the elementary physical education teacher, this handbook offers an exciting range of innovative activities that will reinforce academic learning, strengthen group cooperation skills, and encourage the mastery of those physical education skills so vital for the K to 6 student.

These practical, easy-to-use activities have been organized to provide you with a year 'round source of ideas. Each activity has a recommended grade level, specific educational goals, equipment and materials needed, and easy-to-follow instructions.

The *Elementary Teacher's Handbook of Indoor and Outdoor Games* is divided into eight well-organized chapters for your convenience:

- Chapter 1, "Classroom Games and Icebreakers," offers a selection of special getting-to-know-you activities. Because learning is a sharing experience, these activities will encourage your students to become interested participants in this sharing adventure.

- Chapter 2, "Rainy Day Games," presents exciting indoor activities to change your limited spaces into fun and active places. These activities require little advance preparation and a minimum of classroom set-up. Many will reinforce language arts, mathematics, social studies, and other academic areas. Listening skills, reading readiness activities, and other perceptual-motor suggestions are also included.

- Chapter 3, "Alternative Outdoor Sports and Games," offers a helpful addition to the traditional team sports of basketball, football, and softball. These alternative games provide a refreshing look to nonthreatening and cooperative activities for the elementary child.

- Chapter 4, "Un-Games," is an extension of Chapter 3. Its basic premise is that games should be enjoyed by all children. These special games eliminate no one, are cooperative in nature, and encourage positive social interactions. High student interest and participation are characteristics of these games.

- Chapter 5, "Relays for the Classroom and for Outdoors," contains a variety of indoor and outdoor activities for nonstop relay fun. Relays can serve as excellent warm-up activities and provide novel ways to reinforce movement skills. The chapter also includes suggestions for additional academic tie-in ideas for your use.

- Chapter 6, "Lead-Up Games and Other Activities," will provide your students with a series of progressive games that encourage the mastery of fundamental team-sport skills. These "lead-up" activities offer a gradual approach to skill acquisition, ensuring a more successful experience for your students.

- Chapter 7, "Stunts, Pyramids, and Other Challenges," presents special stunts, contests, and other feats that will challenge your students. Tumbling skills, stunts with partners, fun classroom activities, and other group challenges are also included.

- Chapter 8, "Innovative and Creative Activities," offers a special supplement of new and exciting activities. Parachute games, fun Frisbee® ideas, interesting scooter-board fitness games, and homemade physical education equipment suggestions will provide your students with hours of indoor and outdoor pleasure.

Learning about oneself is a lifetime practice. Our students' ultimate knowledge, attitude, self-expression, and physical skill depend largely on their elementary school and childhood experiences.

The feelings of success, ability, and self-esteem may be the most valuable gifts we can give our students, for they are tools that can be used to shape the future. This book will help you achieve that goal.

Art Kamiya

Contents

Chapter 3 ALTERNATIVE OUTDOOR SPORTS AND GAMES **53**

Chapter 6 LEAD-UP GAMES AND OTHER ACTIVITIES 137

Chapter 7 STUNTS, PYRAMIDS, AND OTHER CHALLENGES 167

Scooter Board Games and Activities

Games to Play on a Limited Budget

chapter ONE

Classroom Games
and Icebreakers

This chapter is filled with over a dozen icebreakers and special "getting-to-know-you" activities that are helpful during those first awkward days of school when your students are starting to build up their early peer relationships. By using a series of nonthreatening classroom games, you can provide your students with interesting and fun ways to get to know each other.

Many of the activities in Chapter 1 can also be used to help inject your class with a quick burst of energy. These "energizers" can actually help your students learn by providing a short physical activity between long periods of academic work. They serve as "pressure-release valves" and bring about renewed ability to concentrate on the important tasks at hand.

As an added feature, all the games in this chapter have been designated as "active learning" ideas. Not only do they provide a physical outlet, but they also reinforce important academic and affective domain skills.

Many of the activities can be used to supplement math concepts and such spatial concepts as *up, down, over,* and *under.* There are many activities that enhance a stronger body image and self-concept, as well as activities that can help your younger students with color and shape recognition.

Thus, Chapter 1 offers the best of both worlds—games that are physically active, have high student interest, and that are fun and provide different ways to practice those important academic skills.

people to people (k-3)

Body Awareness: identifying body parts
Equipment: none

Procedure: This is one of the most exciting indoor activities I know. Not only is it a good icebreaker, but you can use it as a quick class energizer.

The students are divided into pairs. For younger children, it might be easier to pair the students up yourself, but for older ones this can be accomplished quickly by challenging each youngster in the class to find a person to shake hands with.

"Everyone has five seconds to find a person and shake hands!"

Once everyone has a partner, the students must listen to your commands and react to them as quickly as possible. You will then tell them various things to do, using the different parts of the body as cues.

"All partners touch right hand to right hand!"

"Back to back!"

"Knee to knee!"

"Toes to toes!"

On the command "People to people!" each student must quickly find another partner and get back to back with the new partner. The game will then continue with the

3

teacher calling out different commands and the students responding. The timely use of calling out "people to people!" adds to the excitement of the activity.

In circumstances where you have an odd number of students, the person who is left without a partner can become the rover. The rover stands by your side as you call out the commands. Whenever you call "people to people," the rover will try and get a partner. The person who is then left without a partner becomes the new rover.

my ship is loaded (k-3)

Cognitive Awareness: auditory memory sequencing
Equipment: one ball per group

Procedure: All the students are seated in a circle formation. One student starts the activity by rolling the ball to another student, saying, "My ship is loaded with bananas" (or any other cargo he wishes).

The second player receiving the ball has to repeat what the first student said and add another item to the list. "My ship is loaded with bananas and cups." She then rolls the ball to another player. Each player who receives the ball has to repeat what the other players have said and add another item.

When a child fails to repeat all the cargo, the ball is given to the player on his right as the game continues.

This activity can be played with the entire class sitting in a large circle, or you can divide the class into smaller groups. I have found that older students usually enjoy the smaller groups, while younger students find they enjoy the larger group best.

Besides encouraging student interaction, this game can also be used to help your students in learning the names of the other children in the class.

Instead of saying an object, the first person says his name. The other students that receive the ball must repeat all the names given.

Additional Learning Suggestions: This activity can also be applied to the older child learning basic math facts. The first student says a number from one to five. Each additional student who receives the ball will either say an additional number or the sum of the numbers according to the chant given below:

First Player:	(Says number from one to five and rolls ball to second player.)
Everyone:	Plus.
Second Player:	(Says number from one to five and rolls ball to third player.)
Everyone:	Equals.
Third Player:	(Says the sum of the first two numbers, repeats the sum of the two numbers, and rolls ball to fourth player.)
Everyone:	Plus.
Fourth Player:	(Says number from one to five and rolls ball to another player.)
Everyone:	Equals.
Fifth Player:	(Says the sum of the two numbers and repeats the sum.)

This continues until the group reaches the number ninety-nine. The student that says either the number ninety-nine or over will be the new leader as the game starts again.

the machine (k-3)

Social Awareness: group interaction
Equipment: none
Procedure: This activity is a terrific combination of sight and sound. In this game, one person starts as the first part of a huge machine. This student does a certain action and along with this action makes a certain sound. The following students try to join the first student by making actions and sounds that go along with the first student's actions. One by one, the other students become new parts in the growing machine.

After all the students have become parts of the machine, the machine will start to go faster and faster. The sounds and actions of the students become louder and quicker.

The teacher tries to keep the machine running smoothly. She runs around the machine, frantically pumping oil into the machine so it won't overheat.

But it's too late. The machine starts to overheat and with a loud "Boom!" the machine quietly folds up into a pile of tired parts.

name match game (k-3)

Cognitive Awareness: beginning word sounds
Equipment: none

Procedure: Divide your class into smaller groups of five or six players. Arrange them in a circle.

One student starts the game by saying her first name and an object that begins with the same letter as her last name. For example, the first player could say: "Hi, I'm Elizabeth Elephant." Then the person to her left could say: "Glad to meet you, Elizabeth Elephant. My name is Travis Toothache."

This continues around the circle, with each student saying his name and repeating the names of the others.

Other match names can be used. For example the last names could be foods—Billy Bologna, Frances Fish, Susie Syrup.

Or sounds—Sammy Slam, Betty Bong, Artie Arrgh.

Additional Learning Suggestions: You can use this name picture to help your students with some of the important school rules. For younger students, you might want to have them tell you how Sammy Share would act. Or Telly Tattletail. What would be a good name for a person who pushes in line? Many of the kindergarten teachers use similar made-up characters to help their students to remember good cafeteria manners.

For older students, this might make an interesting assignment: "Make up three different characters who could help us to remember good bus safety rules."

beep! time's up (k-3)

Cognitive Awareness: following auditory commands
Equipment: none

Procedure: This is a class challenge activity. Your students will be challenged to perform certain tasks before you count to ten.

For example: "Everyone has ten seconds to touch something hard." After the ten seconds are up, you announce: "Beep! Sorry, time's up!" Then another class challenge is commanded.

While this game can be played indoors, it is best played outside.

Some challenges can be:

"Touch a person wearing red."

"Find something very small."

"Touch something green."

"Touch something that is living."

"Touch your nose to something yellow."

"Shake hands with at least three people."

"Skip to something made of bricks."

"Run to the tree and back."

Additional Learning Suggestions:

1. This activity is good for teaching many of the basic spatial concepts as well as color and shape recognition.

You can make various shapes out of different colored construction paper. They can then be placed on the ground, and the following commands can be given:

"Touch a *red triangle*."

"Jump *over* a *square*."

"Walk *around* a *small square*."

"Touch a *big blue circle*."

"Stand to the *side* of a *green* shape."

"Touch a shape with your *left* hand."

"Touch a *yellow* shape with your *right* foot."

"Put your hand *under* a *red* shape."

Other commands could include the following words: "in front of," "behind," "opposite," "to the left side of," "touch the corner of," "stand in the middle of," and "stand between."

2. For older children, this activity can be made into a math challenge. Place a set of flash cards on the ground. The students then have ten seconds to correctly touch the answers to the following questions with their hands:

"What is two times five?"

"What is seven times nine?"

"Eight divided into sixteen is _____ ?"

"The square root of eighty-one is _____ ?"

"What is the remainder of six divided into fourteen?"

how do you do? (k-3)

Cognitive Awareness: recognizing left and right
Equipment: none

Procedure: All the students are seated in a circle with one student, the Leader, standing in the center. This person approaches one of the players and asks, "How do you do?"

"I'm fine, thank you," is the reply.

"Who are your neighbors?"

If the person cannot name the student next to him in the circle, he must change places with the student in the center. If he does answer correctly, the Leader asks further: "How is Mr. _____ ?" meaning one of the players to the person's right or left.

If the answer is "All right," all the students shift one seat to the right. If the answer is "He's feeling left out," all the students shift one seat to the left. The answer, "All mixed up" allows all of the students to move to any seat they wish. While all this takes place, the Leader will attempt to get into a vacant seat. The person left without a seat is the new Leader.

pocket scavenger hunt (k-3)

Social Awareness: personal interests
Equipment: none

Procedure: Besides allowing the students to interact with each other, this game may also bring some new insight into what your children's interests are.

The teacher has a list of common items children may have in their pockets. As this list is read, the students who have the items hunt through their pockets to retrieve them. The first person to hold the object up is the winner. Points can be awarded to individuals or to groups. Dividing the class in half, using rows as teams, or separating girls and boys are common ways to devise teams.

A sample list may include: Paper clip, pencil, pen, stamp, coin, penny dated before 1970, wallet, picture of a friend, picture of a member of your family, green piece of paper (not money), something made from rubber, piece of lint, an empty pocket, nail file, magnifing glass, magnet, rubber band, marble, golf ball, souvenir from an amusement park, old tooth, lucky rabbit's foot, bottle cap, lock, car key, toy, or mirror.

animal farm surprise (k-up)

Cognitive Awareness: auditory and visual skills
Equipment: ten paper stars and ten paper triangles hidden in classroom

Procedure: For this exciting team treasure hunt activity, divide the class into two groups. Assign a leader to each group. The object is for the members of each group to try and find the hidden paper objects.

    The name of the first group is the Cows. Whenever a member of this group spots a triangle, she starts to moo and point her nose in the direction of the triangle. Other Cows can then join in and point to the hidden triangle. The loud mooing from the Cows alerts the leader of the Cows to find the hidden triangle. The leader then picks up the paper triangle as the rest of the Cows look for other triangle objects. Only the leaders are allowed to pick up the objects.

    In the same manner, the second group is called the Sheep. Whenever a member of the Sheep group spots a hidden paper star, he starts to baa and point his nose in the direction of the star. The Sheep leader then comes and gathers the paper star.

    The first group to find all of its hidden objects is the winner.

    The game can be played again with the Sheep becoming the Cows and the Cows becoming the Sheep. Pick several students to hide the objects while the rest of the class close their eyes. The hidden objects should have a small part showing so they can be spotted by the groups.

Additional Learning Suggestions: Here are additional ideas that reinforce math, historic events, and alphabetical skills.

1. For younger students you can start the activity by having thirteen stars and thirteen triangles, each with a letter of the alphabet on them. When the class has found all the objects, the twenty-six letters can be placed in alphabetical order. Each child can be given a letter, and he walks up to the blackboard and places his letter in the correct order as the class recites the entire alphabet. By using tape, you can stick the letters on the board as each child walks up.

2. This activity could also be used as a part of a history unit. You can use thirteen stars and thirteen stripes to hide. Each stripe has the name of one of the thirteen colonies on it. The stars have the capitols of the thirteen states on them. Instead of Cows and Sheep, you can divide your class into Minutemen and Redcoats. The Minutemen can say, "The British are coming!" and the Redcoats can respond with "Long live the Queen!"

3. This activity can also be used as a math-matching game. The math questions can be placed on the triangles and the correct answers can be written on the stars. After the class has found the hidden objects, the math problems can be reviewed by having students match up the correct answers with the problems.

This type of matching concept has a variety of applications such as matching the names of the presidents with their vice presidents and matching the names of the chemical elements with their symbols. The list of creative ways to use this activity is almost without end.

the "me" package (3-up)

Social Awareness: social interaction and self-disclosure
Equipment: one index card and one pencil per student

Procedure: In this activity each student has to write down three objects that she would like to place in a package. These three objects should be carefully picked so as to reflect some of the characteristics of the student.

For example, you may like to read. So you would send a copy of your favorite book.

Since only three objects can be sent, encourage your students to take some time in considering what three objects they would send.

After all the students have selected their three objects, they write them on their index card. They then stand up and start to walk around the room holding their cards so that the other students can see them. During this time the students are not allowed to talk. When you signal, "Stop!" each student can ask another student standing nearby why he listed a certain object on his paper. Allow them about thirty seconds to exchange information. They will then be told to quietly start walking again. After about eight "Stop!" signals, have the students return to their seats.

It is amazing how quickly this activity can bring your class closer together. Your students will be surprised to find out that they have many similar interests.

time limit bingo (3-up)

Social Awareness: social interaction
Equipment: paper and pencil for each student

Procedure: This activity is quick and simple and encourages student interaction. Each student is given a sheet of paper. The paper is then folded into sixteen squares. The object of the activity is to try and gather as many signatures as possible. Each signature must be clearly written in one of the squares.

Give your class about ten minutes to collect their signatures from the other students. When all sixteen spaces have been filled, the students return to their seats. Now the second part of this activity can begin: Bingo.

Using the class-roll sheet, call off each student's name to the class. Have the student stand up and tell the class a little about herself—name, age, favorite color, or a special interest. Then each student who has that person's signature on his paper will mark off that name on his sheet.

The first person to get four in a row is the winner.

Continue playing until all your students have introduced themselves.

Remember to encourage your students to write their names neatly and clearly.

who stole the cookies? (3-up)

Cognitive Awareness: rhythm and audio perception
Equipment: none

Procedure: This is a chanting activity. It is combined with certain hand motions.

The Leader begins: slap knees . . . clap hands . . . snap right hand . . . snap left hand.

This is used to establish a rhythm for the chant.

The rest of the students are seated in a circle. They all do the motions with the Leader.

> *Leader:* Who stole the cookies from the cookie jar?
> (Student's name) stole the cookies from the cookie jar!
> *Student:* Who me? (One hand snaps.)
> Couldn't be! (One hand snaps.)
> *Student:* (Another student's name) stole the cookies from the cookie jar.

The next student will repeat the chant and name another student. This will continue with every student getting a chance to play.

unfinished sentences (3-up)

Social Awareness: likes and dislikes
Equipment: paper and pencil for each student

Procedure: Using the following list of unfinished sentences, allow your students the chance to finish them as they would like. You can either read the sentences to the class or use a ditto.

I like people who _____ .

If I had one thing I could change about myself it would be _____ .

If I had five dollars I would _____ .

One thing that scares me is _____ .

Sometimes I wish I could _____ .

When I am happy I _____ .

The things that make me sad are _____ .

I want to have a _____ .

My mother always keeps telling me _____ .

I think I always look _____ .

I like to _____ .

I admire _____ .

When people look at me _____ .

When I grow up I want to be a _____ .

The most important person to me is _____ .

I would like to be more _____ .

I think three things that are important to me are _____ .

The funniest thing I ever saw was _____ .

If I had one more day of summer vacation I would _____ .

Whenever I see a fight I feel like _____ .

I like it when people _____ .

Someday I am going to _____ .

Remember to leave some time at the end of this activity to discuss the various answers and remarks from your students.

handful of beans (3-up)

Cognitive Awareness: math facts of odd/even and addition
Equipment: ten to fifteen beans per student

Procedure: The purpose of this activity is to help your students to interact with the other members of the class. It can be used to re-energize your class after a vacation, or as a game to help break the ice.

After the students receive the beans, they can walk around the room. Whenever two students want to, they can enter into the opportunity to play. One student offers a closed hand to the other. In his hand are a number of beans. "Odd or even?" he asks. If the other player answers correctly, she gets the beans. If she answers incorrectly, she must give up that number of beans to the other student.

The aim of the game is to see how many beans one can collect during the course of the game. Ten to fifteen minutes usually makes a good game.

huh? (4-up)

Social Awareness: dealing with a visual handicap
Equipment: none

Procedure: This game is one of a kind. All your students start the game by closing their eyes. One person in the group is then quietly selected by you to be the Leader. You can tap this person on the shoulder as you walk around the group. Once the Leader is selected, he should not do anything to give any clues that he is the Leader. The rest of the students will be told to keep their eyes closed and slowly walk around the room.

Whenever two students meet, they say "Huh?" to each other. The Leader, however, does not talk. Therefore, when a student meets the Leader and asks "Huh?" the Leader will remain quiet. The student who has found the Leader can now open her eyes and line up behind the Leader. Slowly the line of students behind the Leader will grow. Each student should hold on to the student in front of him. When everyone has found the Leader the game is finished.

Remember that only the Leader can remain silent. All the students lined up behind the Leader must still say "Huh?" if they are touched by another student. It is interesting to see the students bump into the Leader's tail. Students will go down the line saying "Huh?" until they reach the Leader.

This activity can be expanded to include an exploration of the feelings the students had while they had their eyes closed. Was it hard for them to walk around the room? How did it feel not to be able to see during this activity? How many of them peeked? Why?

chapter TWO

Chapter 2 offers many indoor activities that will provide endless hours of entertainment for your students. As a classroom teacher, there are many times during the day when you need high-interest activities that can be played in limited areas. Not only are activities in this chapter fun indoors, but they also need a minimum of advance preparation and classroom setup. No matter what your classroom situation, here are activities to help you deal with the problems of limited space.

So, the next time it starts to rain and your students turn gloomy, just bring out a few of these activities.

who's missing? (k-1)

Cognitive Awareness: visual memory
Equipment: none

Procedure: This game is a nice one to play once the students have been together for a few months. The class can be seated at their desks or on the floor in a group. One player is selected to be the Guesser and leaves the room for a few moments.

One player is picked to be the missing person. She will hide behind a bookshelf or door so that when the Guesser returns she will not be seen by the Guesser.

The Guesser has to try to guess which student is missing from the group. If the Guesser is having a hard time figuring out who is missing, the missing player can give a clue to help.

"I sound like this."

"I wear glasses."

"I like the color blue."

body part movement (k-1)

Body Awareness: identifying body parts
Equipment: record player; records; body part cards

Procedure: Have fun with body part movement. Select a record with a nice, easy beat to it. The members of your class will move their body parts to the beat of the music as a certain body part card is shown by the Leader. The body part cards are pictures of the different body parts that have been drawn on poster board. Pictures of arms, hands, head, shoulders, feet, legs, eyes, hips, nose, fingers, and elbows should be drawn on each of the cards.

eraser tag (k-2)

Body Awareness: balance
Equipment: two chalkboard erasers

Procedure: This is another activity that has lasted through many school generations. Here the boys are usually on one team and the girls are on the other. Of course, it doesn't make any difference how the students are divided. One member from each team starts off with balancing an eraser on his head. One of these two players is the Chaser and the other is the Runner. The Chaser tries to touch the Runner without letting the eraser fall off her head. If the Chaser touches the Runner she scores one point for her team. The Chaser also scores one point if the Runner's eraser falls off. The Runner tries to elude the

Chaser as long as possible in the hope that the Chaser's eraser will fall off in the process. If this happens, a point is scored for the Runner's team.

When a point is scored two other players are given a turn to play. Allow each team to alternate the roles of the Chaser and Runner. The play continues until every student has had the opportunity to be involved in the game.

the queen's headache (k-2)

Cognitive Awareness: auditory perception
Equipment: none

Procedure: One student is selected to be the Queen. She sits in the middle of the room on a chair. The rest of the class is lined up on one side of the room.

The object of the game is to quietly get from one side of the room to the other without having the Queen moan. The Queen has such a bad headache that any sound makes her moan. One by one, the students walk across the room. If the Queen hears the student and moans, that student must sit down at the spot where he was when the Queen moaned. The Queen should have her face covered so as to not be accused by the players of showing royal favoritism.

After all the students have had a turn, choose another King or Queen to start the game again.

This is a game that can be used from time to time whenever you need that added reassurance that your classroom *can* be quiet.

Variations: Give one of the following stunts to the students in your class who find it easy to be quiet walkers.

1. Walk with a book balanced on their head.
2. Walk with their shoes tied together.
3. Walk holding one foot with the opposite hand.

i see (k-2)

Body Awareness: movement of different body parts
Equipment: none

Procedure: This is an interesting imitation activity for the entire class. The game begins with the teacher saying: "I see!" The entire class stops what they are doing and responds: "What do you see?" The teacher tells the class what to pretend to do. The students will act out that idea until the teacher says: "I see." All the students stop again and respond: "What do you see?"

The game continues with the teacher suggesting another idea.

SUGGESTIONS

"I see children hopping all around."

"I see walnuts rolling on the ground."

"I see an old person chopping down a tree."

"I see many children laughing at me."

"I see cowboys riding horses high."

"I see insects flying in the sky."

"I see rockets zooming to the moon."

"I see children singing a silent tune."

"I see children quietly sitting down."

"I see people marching 'round the town."

This can be used as a warm-up activity. You can call out ideas that move from slow activities to very active ones, from slow stretching motions to fast movements. By using a command similar to "I see students walking quietly to their chairs," you can easily end the game in a most effective way.

40 ways to get there (k-2)

Body Awareness: moving through space
Equipment: none

Procedure: This can be used as a quick activity for a simple change of pace. All the students are seated. Each child is given a chance to cross the room in a unique and different manner. Once one student has crossed the room in a certain way, no other student is allowed to use that movement. Encourage the use of interesting methods of moving. Any form of locomotion is correct for this game.

ring, bell, ring! (k-2)

Cognitive Awareness: auditory perception
Equipment: one small bell

Procedure: One student is selected to be It. That person stands in front of the rest of the class. Another person is given the bell. This is done in such a fashion that It does not know who has the bell. It can either have his eyes closed or have his back to the students. The person with the bell will ring it a few times while It has his back to the class. It then has to turn around and try to guess who has the bell. If the guess is incorrect, It turns his back again as the bell is rung another time. It has only three chances to guess the student who has the bell. The person with the bell becomes the new leader if It is incorrect three times.

If It correctly selects the student with the bell, another student is given the bell for the next game.

the lost children (k-2)

Cognitive Awareness: visual memory
Equipment: none

Procedure: One student is selected to be the Policeman or Policewoman and leaves the room. Each student has about one minute to change seats with another person in the room. After all the students have been rearranged, the Policeperson is allowed back into the room.

"The children are lost. Please take them back to their homes," says the teacher. The Policeperson then has three minutes to try and get all the students back to their own seats.

Before this game is tried, have students remove personal items or other clues from their own desks.

This activity is a good one to use at the end of the year when your students' desks are usually clean and free of name tags. A wonderful activity for the last day of class!

questions and answers (k-2)

Cognitive Awareness: language arts and body movement
Equipment: none

Procedure: A good indoor activity that can cross over into language arts skills. The students are in their seats. The teacher makes up a question using a child's name and an action word. For example: "Can Jeremy jump on his left foot four times?" The class has to turn the question into a statement. "Jeremy can jump on his left foot four times." The child whose name was called then has to do that activity statement. Allow every student a chance.

cat and mouse tag (k-2)

Body Awareness: moving slowly and quietly through space
Equipment: none

Procedure: This is an activity very similar to Dog and Bone. One student is selected to be the Cat. The Cat sits at the front of the class with her back to the class. The teacher picks four or five students to be the Mice. The band of Mice quietly sneak up to the Cat's chair and start to scratch it. The Cat will then try and tag as many Mice as she can. The first Mouse tagged becomes the new Cat. Select the Mice from different rows to minimize too many Mouse-wrecks. The Mice cannot run between desks, but have to run through the aisles. Cutting through desks can cause the students to trip and fall.

tornado! (k-2)

Cognitive Awareness: learning directions to help with map-reading skills
Equipment: none

Procedure: The leader stands in front of the class. The rest of the students stand behind their desks. The leader says: "The wind blows east." All the other students must then face toward the east. The leader can say any one of the four directions and the rest of the class is to turn toward that direction. Students who do not turn to the correct direction are not eliminated from the activity, but encourage them to listen and think before they point in the desired direction. When the leader shouts: "Tornado!" all the students must turn around one time and sit down as quickly as possible.
    The first player to sit down becomes the new leader.

Variations: This activity can also be used as a team game. Each of the rows in the class is a team. The teacher is the leader. When the teacher calls: "Tornado!" the first row to sit down receives one point. The first team to get five points is the winner.

do this, do that (k-2)

Body Awareness: identifying body parts
Equipment: none

Procedure: This game is one of the many variations of Simon Says.
    The leader stands in front of the class. She makes body movements while saying either "Do this" or "Do that." When she says "Do this," the class has to move their bodies and duplicate her action. If she says "Do that," the class should not do that action. This is an interesting game, with the leader trying to fool the class and the rest of the class trying to remain alert and not make any errors.
    After a certain time period, change the leader.

Variation: Another game that is appropriate for the primary grades is Touch Your Head. In this activity, the teacher says "Touch your head" or any other body part. The teacher also touches her head at the same time.
    When the teacher wants to trick the class, she will say "Touch your feet" and instead of touching her feet she touches her nose. Some of the students will touch their nose instead of their feet. Encourage the students to *listen* to what you say before they do that action.

duke of york (k-2)

Cognitive Awareness:　using word opposites
Equipment:　none

Procedure:　This is a fun singing activity. You can use the following words to any tune you want. The students are sitting down on chairs or on the ground.

> *There was a Duke of York,*
> *He had ten thousand men,*
> *He marched them up the hill,* (students all stand up)
> *And he marched them down again.* (students sit down)
> *'Cause when you're up, you're up,* (students stand up)
> *And when you're down you're down,* (students sit down)
> *And when you're only halfway up,* (students stand halfway up)
> *You're neither up nor down!* (students quickly stand up and sit down)

This activity can further explore other word opposites such as: soft and hard, east and west, hot and cold, and on and off. I have found that older students enjoy this activity if the song is sung faster and faster. It then becomes a challenge to keep up with the leader.

Try doing this song backwards! Offer your students the opportunity to try and do the song by doing the opposite movements. If they were to stand up, then they have to sit down when they hear the word "up." It's interesting to see how many students have a hard time getting used to this opposite concept.

To start this activity the students all stand up before beginning to sing.

seat circle exchange (k-2)

Body Awareness:　distinguishing left from right
Equipment:　none

Procedure:　This activity is best done with eight to twelve students in a group. The students arrange their seats to form a tight circle. One member of the group is selected to stand in the center of the circle. The object of the game is for the player in the center to sit down in an empty seat as soon as possible. The other players in the circle try and keep the center player from finding a seat by moving quickly from seat to seat in a given direction. The teacher indicates which way the group is to move. The group moves in that direction trying to keep the vacant seat from being sat in by the player in the center. The teacher can tell the group to move either left or right and can change the direction at any time during the activity. When the player in the center sits in the vacant seat, another player is selected to be the person in the center.

While this activity can reinforce the concepts of left and right in the lower grades, upper elementary children just enjoy the game because of its fast action and energetic fun. You can also add another command by saying: "Mix up." This command tells the students that they must quickly find another seat. When this is done, the last player to find a seat is the new player in the center.

20 sounds (k-2)

Cognitive Awareness: sound discrimination
Equipment: a bed sheet; various objects that have a distinctive sound when dropped such as a bell, a key, a plastic cup

Procedure: The various objects are dropped one at a time to the floor from behind the sheet. The students are then asked what object they think has been dropped after the teacher gives them the choices of the items that were dropped.

You can have the students close their eyes to help them better focus on listening for the sounds.

When the activity is played with older students, you can have them write down what they think was dropped. After the twenty objects have been dropped, you can remove the sheet and drop the items over again. The player with the most correct answers is the winner.

poor kitty (k-2)

Social Awareness: group interaction
Equipment: none

Procedure: The students are seated in a circle. One of the students is selected to be the Kitty. The Kitty will sit in the center of the circle. As the Kitty sits in the center he will purr and frequently say "meow." The Kitty will go up to the first student and purr and meow. The first student has to pet the kitty on its head and say "Poor Kitty, poor Kitty, poor Kitty," without laughing or making a sound. If a player makes a sound she is out of the game for a short while. Kitty will then go on to the next player and meow. The Kitty will try and make each student laugh or make any sound by saying "meow" in different and funny ways.

For older students, you can have the rule that anyone who laughs has to exchange places with the Kitty. This works well for students in grades four to six. The students in the younger grades all want to be the Kitty and so it's hard to have this rule at that age level.

head, shoulders, knees, and toes (k-2)

Body Awareness: identifying body parts
Equipment: none

Procedure: This is an activity song. As the Leader sings the song he will touch certain body parts. The rest of the class has to follow the actions of the Leader as he sings:

> *Head, shoulders, knees, and toes,*
> *Knees and toes.*
> *Head, shoulders, knees, and toes,*
> *Knees and toes.*
> *Oh, eyes and ears and mouth and nose.*
> *Head, shoulders, knees and toes,*
> *Knees and toes!*

The Leader and the rest of the class touch the various body parts as the song is sung. On the second verse the students do not say the word "head" and instead will only touch the head instead of saying the word. This will continue for the words "shoulders," "knees," and "toes."

dog and bone (k-3)

Cognitive Awareness: auditory perception
Equipment: one chalkboard eraser

Procedure: One child is selected to be the Dog. He sits in front of the rest of the students with his eyes closed and his back to the class. The bone lies next to the Dog's chair. Silently, the teacher will signal for a student to try and get the bone. If the Dog hears the student, the dog says: "Bow, wow." The student then has to sit down. Another student is selected by the teacher to try and sneak up on the Dog and steal his bone. A student who successfully touches the bone becomes the next Dog as the game continues.

Variations: This activity can also be converted into a tag game. The Dog stands with his back to the rest of the students. If the Dog thinks someone is approaching, he turns around and tries to tag the student. If the student touches the bone or gets back to his seat, he is safe. If the Dog tags him before this is done, the student becomes the Dog.

This activity is fun if you allow unequal time periods between attempts. This will throw the Dog off and cause him to turn around. If the Dog turns around and no one has left his seat, the Dog has to let someone else take his place. The teacher will silently pick the student to attempt to get to the bone. Encourage class cooperation and fair play to maintain silence during this game.

knots (k-3)

Cognitive Awareness: spatial concepts of *up, over, under, above,* and others
Equipment: none

Procedure: One student is selected to be the Leader. This student leaves the room for a moment. The rest of the students form a circle by holding each others' hands. They try to tangle up the circle by stepping over, under, and through the arms and legs of others. While the students are making these knots in the circle, they cannot let go of their hands. The Leader then comes back into the room and tries to untangle the students into the original circle. The Leader instructs each tangled player as to the exact movements that each must do to become untangled. For example:

"David, please step over Sally's arm."

"Elaine, please turn and face this way . . . now go under Ricky's left arm."

The game continues with another student selected as the Leader and the group becoming tangled once again.

audience storytime (k-3)

Cognitive Awareness: listening for verbal cues
Equipment: none

Procedure: The students can be seated at their desks or on the floor. Different children are divided into certain groups and given a sound or phrase to say whenever they hear their cue. The teacher reads the story below and the students respond to the story when they hear their special cue word.

CUE WORDS	RESPONSE
Brave Ben	Group claps their hands
Mean Mitchell	Group boos and hisses
Happy Hannah	Group says: "My hero" in a girlish voice.
Baby Bill	Group cries: "Waa, waa"

Once upon a time there lived a young lady called HAPPY HANNAH. HAPPY HANNAH lived in a small run-down shack at the outskirts of the town of Buffalo Trail. One day MEAN MITCHELL came to her house and knocked on the door. Knock, knock, knock!

"Who's that knocking at my door?" asked HAPPY HANNAH.

"It is I, MEAN MITCHELL," came the reply. "I've come to get the back rent that you owe me."

"But, MEAN MITCHELL, I do not have the rent," sadly exclaimed HAPPY HANNAH.

"Well, then I will have to take your small brother, BABY BILL, and sell him!" said MEAN MITCHELL.

"No!" shouted HAPPY HANNAH, "I won't let you take BABY BILL!"

"Well, then," said MEAN MITCHELL with a mean smile, "I'll not take BABY BILL if you marry me."

"Marry you!" said HAPPY HANNAH. "Never!"

But MEAN MITCHELL tore down the door and grabbed the arm of HAPPY HANNAH in one hand and the arm of BABY BILL in the other.

"I'll sell BABY BILL and then marry you!" screamed MEAN MITCHELL.

"Oh, if only BRAVE BEN were here!" cried HAPPY HANNAH.

"Unhand them!" said BRAVE BEN, who had just come in the door.

"Curses, foiled again!" said MEAN MITCHELL.

So MEAN MITCHELL rode off into the sunset while HAPPY HANNAH, BABY BILL, and BRAVE BEN lived happily ever after.

THE END

the magic box (k-up)

Cognitive Awareness: problem solving and role playing
Equipment: one box filled with fifteen to twenty different animal pictures

Procedure: Place the box of pictures on a chair. The students are sitting in a circle a short distance from the Magic Box of pictures. Four or five students are selected by the teacher to be the first group of Actors. One person out of this group is selected to pick a picture from the Magic Box. She shows the picture to the rest of the Actors. After the Actors have seen the animal picture, they return to the center of the group. They then imitate the animal that has been selected. Once the correct animal has been guessed, the Actors return to the circle. The game continues with new Actors.

Variations: When this activity is used with older students, the pictures in the Magic Box can be made appropriate to their interest levels. Transportation pictures of motorcycles, airplanes, people skating, police cars, and other vehicles are of special interest to many students. You can also use pictures of famous people. George Washington could be role played by chopping down a cherry tree. Using pictures of various occupations can also be a source for interesting group role playing.

hide the thimble (k-up)

Social Awareness: group cooperation
Equipment: a small rubber eraser

Procedure: The teacher chooses one student to be the Hunter. The Hunter is sent out of the room while the rest of the class hides the object. When the Hunter re-enters the room, the other students help her in finding the object by humming louder if the Hunter is close to the object. The closer she is to the object, the louder and faster the students are to hum.
   When the Hunter finds the object, another Hunter is picked.

birds fly (k-up)

Cognitive Awareness: classifying by groups
Equipment: none

Procedure: This is an activity that has been around the classroom for generations. All the students stand behind their desks. A Leader stands at the front of the class. He calls out: "Ducks fly, pigs fly, deer fly, eagles fly . . ." When he names an animal that does fly, the rest of the class has to flap their arms in a flying motion. Any child who does not flap his arms when the leader says the name of an animal that flies has made a mistake. This also goes for those students who flap their arms when the leader says an animal that does not fly.
   Encourage students to listen carefully and try not to make mistakes. However, the students who do make errors are not eliminated from the activity. After all, everyone makes mistakes, even teachers.

walking through the jungle (k-up)

Cognitive Awareness: following commands
Equipment: none

Procedure: While this activity is suited for the younger child, I have found that older students really enjoy the fantasy and make-believe actions of this activity too.

This is an activity in which the students must echo your words and actions as they walk through the jungle in search of a wild lion.

The teacher starts by slapping his hands on his knees to establish a slow walking rhythm. The students follow his motions and will repeat his words to this slapping rhythm.

TEACHER	STUDENTS
"Let's go on a lion hunt!"	"Let's go on a lion hunt!"
"OK."	"OK."
"Let's go."	"Let's go."
"Walking through the jungle."	"Walking through the jungle."
"Looking for a lion."	"Looking for a lion."

The students continue to repeat the words and the motions of the teacher as the activity continues.

"Oh, look!" (The teacher points.)
"There's a bridge."
"Let's cross it." (The teacher beats his fists on his chest.)
"Walking through the jungle."
"Looking for a lion."
"Oh, look!" (Teacher points.)
"There's a river."
"Let's swim it." (Teacher makes a swimming motion with his arms.)
"Walking through the jungle."
"Looking for a lion."
"Oh, look!" (The teacher points.)
"There's a puddle."
"Can't go under it."
"Can't swim it."
"Can't jump over it."
"Let's cross it." (Teacher interlocks the fingers of both hands and thumps the palms of his fist together making a sound of boots crossing the puddle.)

"Walking through the jungle."

"Looking for a lion."

"Oh, look!" (Teacher points.)

"There's a field."

"Can't go around it."

"Can't jump it."

"Can't go under it."

"Let's cross it." (Teacher rubs his hands together making the sound of walking through the tall grass.)

"Walking through the jungle."

"Looking for a lion!"

"Oh, look! There's a cave." (Teacher starts to whisper.)

"Be brave . . . in the cave."

"It's dark in here. . . ." (Using a scared voice.)

"It's cold in here."

"It's . . . WOW!!!! What's this?!! (Teacher raises his voice in surprise.)

"It has two eyes." (Teacher motions the lion's face as he touches the different body parts.)

"It has one nose."

"It has hair."

"Sharp teeth."

"And a long tail."

"IT MUST BE A LION! RUN!!" (The teacher quickly slaps his hands against his knees in a running motion. As the children run back through the jungle, the teacher makes the motions of the field, the puddle, the river, and the bridge.)

"Whew! Home at last!"

analogies (k-up)

Cognitive Awareness: finding relationships through analogies
Equipment: none

Procedure: Divide the class into two teams. Using a list of analogies, ask each player if she can solve an analogy. Score one point for a correct answer.

Here is a partial list of common relationships:

1. People:Village as Bees:?	9. Beak:Bird as Snout:?
2. Pen:Writer as Scissors:?	10. Air:Blimp as Water:?

3. Boy:Man as Girl:?
4. Hot:Cold as Small:?
5. Sparrow:Hawk as Minnow:?
6. Peak:Mountain as Head:?
7. Baa:Sheep as Meow:?
8. Beaver:Dam as Man:?

11. Cantilever:Bridge as Swallowtail:?
12. Rib Roast:Chef as Bread:?
13. Wings:Flies as Feet:?
14. Voice:Singer as Piano:?
15. Wood:Carpenter as Bricks:?
16. Fur:Cat as Shell:?

ring on a string (2-up)

Social Awareness:　group cooperation
Equipment:　a long piece of string; a ring

Procedure:　Place the ring on the string so that it can slide back and forth. Tie the string to form a big circle. Have your students stand in a circle. Each student holds the string with two hands. One student stands in the center of the circle. She is the Guesser. The students in the group pass the ring around the circle in such a way that the Guesser cannot see the ring being passed from person to person. The Guesser has three chances to find the ring. If she guesses the person who has the ring, she changes places with that person. After three incorrect guesses, a new Guesser is picked.

bees and snakes (3-up)

Social Awareness:　group cooperation
Equipment:　a chalkboard eraser to represent honey; a pencil to represent a lizard

Procedure: Divide the class into two groups: the Bees and the Snakes. Select one member from each side to be the leaders. The two leaders then go outside the classroom. The remaining students quietly watch as the two objects are hidden somewhere in the classroom. The aim of the game is to help your leader in finding the hidden objects. Each group does this by making a certain sound if their leader is close to their secret object. The Bees make a buzzing noise if their leader is close to the honey (eraser). The Snakes make a hissing sound when their leader starts to get closer to the pencil (lizard).

Encourage the teams to get louder and louder as their leader gets closer to the designated objects. On the other hand, the groups should make less noise when the leaders start to move away from the objects.

The first team to help their leader in finding the hidden object wins.

find the leader (3-up)

Social Awareness: group cooperation
Equipment: none

Procedure: This is an excellent activity to help cure those rainy day doldrums.

Arrange the students in a circle or in a similar arrangement that allows all the students to easily see the rest of the class. The object of this activity is to follow all the movements of the Leader so as to prevent a fellow student from finding the Leader.

One student is selected to be the Guesser. This student leaves the room and waits outside. The rest of the group will try and follow the movements and gestures of a designated Leader in the group. For example, if the Leader puts his right hand on his head, all the other students will try to duplicate this movement at the same time. The

Guesser is brought back into the room and stands in the middle of the group. As the Leader makes his movements and the rest of the group follows, the Guesser has three chances to guess the real Leader.

Encourage the students not to look directly at the Leader as this will easily give the Guesser clues as to who the Leader is. A good class will try and duplicate the exact movements of the Leader as quickly as possible.

When the Guesser picks the Leader, or after three wrong guesses, select other students to take the places of the Guesser and Leader.

the bicycle race (3-up)

Body Awareness: endurance
Equipment: none

Procedure: This is a quick classroom energizer that can bring about amazing results. It can be used for a short change-of-pace activity or as a longer game the whole class can enjoy.

Arrange the desks of the students so that the runners are able to support themselves on the desks as shown in the illustration above. Divide the classroom into two teams. One member from each team is selected to be the Runner. The object of the activity is to stay supported on the desks for as long as possible while pretending to be peddling a bicycle. The student who stays up the longest scores a point for his group. Let every student receive the opportunity to participate.

Variations: Instead of having only two Runners, have four groups participating. In this way, more students will be involved at a time. Award points in the following manner: 4 points for first place, 3 points for second, 2 points for third, and 1 point for fourth place.

A less competitive way to encourage participation is to challenge the entire class to see if they can bicycle for "500 miles." In this activity the class members are divided into four groups. The challenge is for each group to be able to bicycle for a total of "500 miles" or five minutes. This is done in a relay fashion. The first person from each group will try to peddle for as long as possible and as fast as possible. As soon as she gets tired, the second person in the group gets to have his turn. This must continue for the next five minutes. At the end of every minute the teacher can call out: "That's one hundred miles down. Let's get to five hundred!"

Encourage the weaker students to try and peddle for as long as possible. At the same time, remind the other members that this is a group effort. If they all try their best it will be possible for the entire class to contribute to the collective goal of peddling for five minutes. When the five minutes are up, congratulations are in order.

During some point in the school year you might try for a cross-country journey. How long will it take your class to peddle from New York to the sandy shores of California? You can bring an interesting geography lesson into your classroom by learning about the states that would be on your journey as your class peddles 500 miles on each day of your bicycle adventure. A mileage chart could add to the excitement. And of course, a small class party or picnic at the end of the journey would be just the thing to top off a week of rugged bicycling.

20 questions (3-up)

Cognitive Awareness: problem solving through deductive logic
Equipment: none

Procedure: This is an all-time favorite.

One student is selected to be the Leader. The Leader leaves the room for a moment. The rest of the class is told of a secret object. The secret object is an item that is in the room and visible to all.

The Leader then returns to the classroom. The aim of the Leader is to try and deduce what the secret object is by asking questions of the class. The questions must be ones that can be answered by a "yes" or a "no."

For example: Let us say that the secret object is the clock hanging on the front wall. The Leader could ask questions like, "Is it made of wood?" The rest of the class would naturally answer "No." Therefore, the Leader knows that all the items in the classroom that are wooden are to be eliminated.

"Is it made out of metal?" asks the Leader. "Yes!" replies the class.

Now the Leader knows to look for something metal.

This process of questioning goes on and the Leader will be given more and more information as to what the secret object is. The Leader has to try and narrow the characteristics of the object enough so that he can make a good guess as to what the object is.

At last, the Leader is about to find the secret object.

"Is the object on a wall?"	"Yes," replies the class.
"Is it round?"	"Yes."
"Is it moving?"	"Yes."
"Is it made of glass and metal, with arms that move?"	"YES!"
"Is it the CLOCK!"	"Yes!" shouts the class!

Of course, the "no" answers that the class gives may supply just as much information to the Leader as the "yes" answers. If the Leader cannot guess the secret object within 20 questions, the class can give the Leader three clues about the object. Usually that will easily give the object away to the Leader.

This activity is an excellent one for encouraging your students in using deductive logic.

Variations:

1. Try playing the Secret Number Game. This activity is played in a similar manner as twenty questions. The only change is that the class is told of a secret number that is picked from the numbers 0 to 100. The Leader has 20 questions to narrow down the field of numbers to the right secret number. Questions like:

"Is it greater than fifty?"

"Is it an even number?"

"Is it a multiple of seven?"

can be asked. This is a quick activity and many of the Leaders will find it quite easy to guess the number under ten questions.

2. Another way to play this game is to have the teacher think of a secret object. Then, one by one, each student is given the chance to ask one question about the object. After twenty questions, the students write down on a piece of paper what they believe the object to be. This is also a quick activity, and can be used as a short five-to-ten minute activity.

sing down! (3-up)

Cognitive Awareness: language arts through a musical medium
Equipment: one pencil and one piece of paper per group

Procedure: This activity will help to bring some music and rhythm into your class. Divide the class into about five groups. Assign a recording secretary for each group. The object of the activity is for each group to try and come up with songs that have words about the weather in the title or a verse in the song and they are then quickly written down by the secretary. Each group has five minutes to think of as many songs as possible.

After the five minutes are up, each group has to sing at least three stanzas of each song to receive credit. The group that has the most songs correctly sung is the winner.

Examples: "Singin' in the *Rain*," "Frosty the *Snow*man," "*Sunshine* on My *Shoulder*," "Jingle Bells: Dashing Through the *Snow*. . . ."

Any song with words like clouds, hot, foggy, rain, snow, sunny, cold, raindrops, and other weather words is allowed.

As far as we know, the current world record is 34 songs. Try to beat that!

puzzle tile (3-up)

Cognitive Awareness: math facts and other word pairs
Equipment: one sheet of paper, scissors, and pencils for each group

Procedure: Divide your class into groups of three to five players. Each group is given a sheet of paper, a pair of scissors, and a pencil. The paper is folded into eight different sections as shown:

Each group is to make up math problems or word pairs to write on the different edges of the sheet of paper. For example, one group could be asked to write math problems using the four times table, another group is to have word opposites, another group is to have words that sound alike but are spelled differently. Once the puzzle tile is completed, one player cuts the puzzle with the scissors along the folds in the paper. These puzzles are then exchanged with the other groups. Each group is given a certain time limit to finish the eight-piece puzzle. Then the group is given another group's puzzle. Continue this until all the puzzles are seen by every group.

A greater challenge would include the making of a sixteen-square puzzle. Older students will enjoy this activity because of its various combinations of possible solutions.

new year's name resolutions (3-up)

Cognitive Awareness: language arts
Equipment: paper; pencils

Procedure: The students will make several New Year resolutions using the letters of their first name to generate things they feel would be good resolutions.

For example, "Travis" would look like this:

Take out the trash more often.

Rake the leaves in the fall.

Ask permission before leaving the yard.

Visit a sick friend.

Invite my teacher to a steak dinner.

Spend more time keeping my room neat and clean.

Another activity that uses this same method is to have your students think of descriptive words that begin with the letters of their name. Each word should describe the student in positive ways.

"Ann" would be:

Attractive

Nice

Neat

proverb word scramble (3-up)

Cognitive Awareness: language arts
Equipment: paper; pencils

Procedure: Each student has a sheet of paper and a pencil. A certain proverb is written on the blackboard. The students have to think of other words that can be spelled using the letters that appear on the blackboard. The words have to be four letters or longer.

The following proverbs can be used:

A penny saved is a penny earned.

A stitch in time saves nine.

One picture is worth a thousand words.

After a certain time limit, see which students have the most words.

letter people (3-up)

Cognitive Awareness: language arts
Equipment: paper; pencils

Procedure: The object of this activity is to think of various letters of the alphabet that represent words or other things. Each student then makes up a story as to why these letters left the alphabet.

For example, a student could say that there are no longer twenty-six letters in the alphabet because:

E.T. went home, J.R. got shot, the J flew away, the EZ left because life was too hard, and I went home.

Other letter people and items could be:

B: bee
C: see, sea
I-C: icy
I-V: ivy
M-T: empty
D-K: decay

the king's sword (3-up)

Social Awareness: student interaction and group cooperation
Equipment: none

Procedure: Have your students sit in a circle. Each of the students represents a number. One of the students starts off by saying: "Have you seen the King's sword?" as she points to one of the players in the circle.

"Who, sir. Me, sir?" comes the reply from the second student.

"Yes, sir. You, sir," says the first student.

"No, sir. Sorry, sir," says the second student.

"Then who, sir?" continues the first student.

"Number eight, sir," says the second student as he thinks of another student.

The game continues as the first student asks the number-eight student whether he saw the King's sword. Each reply should be quick and rapid, as this adds to the fun of the game.

first name, last name (3-up)

Cognitive Awareness: language arts
Equipment: paper; pencils

Procedure: The students try to match up a letter of the alphabet with the first or last letters of the other students in the class.

They walk around the class and collect the signatures of the other students to fill in their paper.

Example:

A. *Alex Smith*

B. *Brown, Steve*

C. *Chris Castor*

D. *Dawn Hunnicutt*

E. *East, John*

If there are no students with some of the letters of the alphabet, you can fill in with names such as either Miss Ing or Mr. Gone.

anatomy action (3-up)

Cognitive Awareness: scientific terms for body parts
Equipment: none

Procedure: This activity can be used as an introduction to the scientific names of the different body parts. The students have to follow the instructions that are given below and quickly touch or perform the task desired.

Touch your mandible (jaw).

Tap your cranium five times (head).

Rub your patella (knee cap).

Move your phalanges (fingers or toes).

Twist your ilium (hips).

Scratch your scapula (shoulder).

Bend your vertebrae (spine or back).

Beat your sternum (chest).

alphabet hunters (3-up)

Cognitive Awareness: language arts
Equipment: paper; pencils

Procedure: The object of this activity is for each student to try and list objects found in the classroom that begin with the various letters of the alphabet. Each student writes the twenty-six letters down the left-hand side of the paper. Next to that letter the student will list the name of an object found in the classroom that begins with the given letter. After a certain time limit see which students have the most objects listed. You may use this list of items to give examples to your students after the activity is over:

A: alphabet, apple, atlas, air
B: banner, back, bag
C: class, clock, circle
D: dial, desk, dictionary
E: elbow, edge, elastic, ear
F: friend, filmstrip, flag, fork
G: goldfish, gum, globe
H: hat, handle, head, hexagon
I: illustration, India ink, intercom, item
J: jar, jigsaw puzzle, jumper, journal
K: key, knee, kids, knob
L: lamp, lap, leg, lights
M: mask, mess, microscope, motif
N: nose, needle, nut
O: oblong, oil, outline, overalls
P: postcard, pan, paper, plant
Q: questions, quarter, quotation, quill
R: rack, radiator, radio, records
S: screen, seat, shadow, sandwich
T: tile, teeth, trapezoid, typewriter
U: upholstery, umbrella, unit, us
V: vest, ventilator, volumes, venetian blinds
W: window, waist, water, wheel
X: xylophone
Y: yarn, yardstick, you
Z: zipper, zero

common theme word skit (3-up)

Cognitive Awareness: recognizing words of a common theme
Equipment: different word lists

Procedure: Divide your class into groups of six to eight people. Each group is given a list of words on a common theme. For example:

> Words that describe ways to travel: car, train, feet, horse, canoe, helicopter, ski, bus, hang gliding, subway, camel, and skates
>
> Words that describe items that hold or contain things: purse, box, shoes, house, boat, pea pod, mouth, dictionary, bathtub, and a city

The object of the activity is to make up a short skit that contains these words as part of the dialogue. The other groups will quietly listen and try to write down the words they think belong to the common theme. Before each group presents their skit, they must tell the audience what their theme is.

The group with the most correct words is the winner.

the class writers' colony (3-up)

Cognitive Awareness: language arts
Equipment: paper; pencils

Procedure: Each student is given a piece of paper. The students each write the following sentence: "I couldn't believe it, but standing in the front yard of my house was a. . . ." The students then pass their papers to the student to their left. These students finish the original sentence and add another sentence. When they are through, they pass the papers to the next students. This continues until all the students in the class have had a chance to add to each story. When each paper returns to the original owner, he will read the story and give it a title. The teacher can read some of the more interesting stories. The same thing can be done in building a poem. The first player will write one line of poetry. The second player has to add an additional line to the poem. The poem does not have to rhyme, but each student should be encouraged to try and fit each additional line with the general theme of the poem.

Why not try and start your group poem off with the beginning from a familiar poem you have been studying?

contest winners (3-up)

Cognitive Awareness: language arts
Equipment: several magazines

Procedure: The class is divided into several small groups of four to five players. Each group is given two or more ads or contest announcements that have been taken from the magazines. The object of the activity is to use one ad and change it by exchanging words with those from one of the other ads.

For example, an ad about the newest cars could be mixed with one about a cooking contest.

Yes, our latest luxury CHICKENS are just loaded with exciting new options: Power WALNUTS, convertible WINGS, AM/FM WINE SAUCE, and steel-belted STUFFING. Just think, you too could be a proud owner of the streamlined TURKEY! Just drop in to one of our many CHOPPED NUTS for details.

Now you're cooking!

cities and states (3-up)

Cognitive Awareness: geography
Equipment: alphabet flash cards; map of the United States

Procedure: The students can use a map of the United States to help them as they do this activity. The teacher will shuffle the alphabet flash cards and call out the first letter. The students will then try to quickly name a city or state that begins with that letter. If a state is named, the student must also name the states that border it, using the map. If a city is named, the student must tell which state the city is in. If this is done correctly, the teacher gives that student the flash card.

It is continued until all the possible letters are called. The winner is the student with the most flash cards.

calendar shuffleboard (3-up)

Cognitive Awareness: math facts
Equipment: one old calendar; several bottle caps

Procedure: This is a good activity for two to four players. Tape one of the months from the calendar on a long table. From a line about two feet from the calendar the players have to flick their checkers onto the calendar. They score points by landing on the days of the month. The first player or team to score 250 points is the winner.

missing person descriptions (3-up)

Cognitive Awareness: using descriptive words
Equipment: one index card and pencil per player

Procedure: Each player is given an index card. The object of this activity is to write down a series of descriptive words that tell about the students' interests and special talents. Only one physical trait can be listed as a part of this exercise. The cards are then collected and the teacher reads each card one at a time. The rest of the students try to guess which child is the missing person.

buzz (3-up)

Cognitive Awareness: math facts
Equipment: none

Procedure: The class is seated at their desks. The object of the game is to substitute the word "buzz" for the word "seven." The players will each count off one number at a time. The student who has the number seven should say "buzz" instead of seven. The next player will then continue by saying "eight." This will progress around the room with players who have a seven in their number substituting "buzz" for seven.

For example:

17: buzz-teen

27: twenty-buzz

77: buzz-ty-buzz.

Have your class count up to eighty. It's guaranteed to keep your class buzzing!
Another way to play the game is to have the students say "buzz" whenever they have a number that is a multiple of seven. The numbers of 7, 14, 21, 28, . . . will require a "buzz" instead of the number. This can be done for any number desired.

quietball (3-up)

Body Awareness: catching and throwing skills
Equipment: one foam-rubber ball

Procedure: This activity is great for a rainy day! The students stand near their desks. The object of the game is to catch and throw the ball without making the following mistakes:

1. A player is out if he makes any noise.
2. A player is out if she drops the ball or throws the ball so that another player cannot easily get it.

3. A player is out if he throws the ball back to the player who threw it to him.

One student is given the ball to start the action. She throws the ball to any player in the class. The ball is then thrown from player to player at random. All players must keep both feet on the floor. If any of the players make a mistake they must sit down and wait for the next game to begin.

the world traveler (3-up)

Cognitive Awareness: geography
Equipment: pencils; paper; slips of paper with the name of a different city written on each one

Procedure: This activity is a good one to follow up a unit on your state's cities. A sheet of paper is taped to each student's back by the teacher. On a signal, all the students go around the room trying to write down the names of the cities on the other student's backs. The students will twist and turn to prevent the other students from reading their city. After ten minutes the students all sit down. Each player takes the piece of paper off his back and announces the city to the class.

The player with the most cities written down is the winner.

head to toe (3-up)

Cognitive Awareness: drawing a picture from descriptive words
Equipment: drawing paper; pencils

Procedure: The students listen as the teacher describes what a certain creature looks like. As the creature is described, the students draw it.

> The creature has a very fuzzy head and has three eyes and two ears on either side of its head. It has two horns that resemble pine tree branches. It has a long, skinny neck like an ostrich. *NOW* carefully fold the top of your paper over so that only the bottom of the neck shows. Pass the paper to the student on your right. Everyone should have another student's paper.
>
> Now, connected to the neck of the creature is its large body. Its shoulders are wide and bony. It has a fat stomach covered with fur. Its arms are big and long; each hand has eight fingers. *NOW* fold the paper again, leaving a part of the body exposed. Pass the paper to the student on your right.

This type of description continues for the legs and feet of the creature. When the last students are finished with their drawings, the picture is given to the original student. He can then unfold the paper and see what the creature looks like.

united states roll call (3-up)

Cognitive Awareness: reviewing the names of the fifty states
Equipment: pencils; paper

Procedure: While this may sound easy, challenge your class to name all the fifty states. Give your class about fifteen minutes to write down as many states as they can. After the time limit is up, name all the fifty states.
     The student with the most correct states is the winner.

vowels in sports (3-up)

Cognitive Awareness: problem solving and language arts
Equipment: pencils; paper

Procedure: Place the following mystery words on the blackboard. The words are names of sports with only the vowels of each sport indicated. Have the students to fill in the blanks.

1. _ A _ _ E _ _ A _ _ (Basketball)
2. _ E _ _ I _ (Tennis)
3. _ _ I _ _ I _ _ (Swimming)
4. _ A _ E _ A _ _ (Baseball)
5. _ O _ _ E _ (Soccer)
6. _ OO _ _ A _ _ (Football)
7. _ O _ _ (Golf)
8. _ O _ _ I _ _ (Bowling)
9. _ _ II _ _ (Skiing)
10. _ U _ _ I _ _ (Surfing)
11. A _ _ _ E _ _ (Archery)
12. _ A _ _ UE _ _ A _ _ (Racquetball)
13. _ O _ _ E _ _ A _ _ (Volleyball)
14. _ O _ O (Polo)
15. _ A _ _ I _ _ O _ (Badminton)
16. I _ E _ _ A _ I _ _ (Ice Skating)
17. _ A _ _ _ A _ _ (Handball)
18. _ _ A _ _ (Track)

paper bag self-portrait (3-up)

Social Awareness: self-disclosure in a group
Equipment: paper bags; markers; scissors

Procedure: Each student is given a paper bag and a marker. The paper bag is placed over the student's head. Using the marker, the student tries to draw a face on the paper bag while it is on his head. After the eyes have been drawn, the student can remove the bag and take a pair of scissors to cut out two circles for his eyes. Each student should try and have as much detail in his drawing as possible.

A good follow-up activity would be for each of the students to go to the front of the class and see how many of the students can guess who is who.

A sheet can be placed around the body of each mystery student to avoid clues from the student's clothing.

teapot (3-up)

Cognitive Awareness: problem solving through the use of various clues
Equipment: none

Procedure: This activity is directed by a Leader who stands at the front of the class. The object of the game is for the students to try and guess the secret word the Leader will be using in several sentences.

For example, the secret word is "wish." As the Leader is asked questions about the secret word, she will answer them by substituting the word TEAPOT with the secret word.

> *Student #1:*   Is the secret word an object?
>
> *Leader:*   No, it's not an object, but I often TEAPOT it were.
>
> *Student #2:*   Is it a verb?
>
> *Leader:*   Yes, but you can TEAPOT anywhere.
>
> *Student #3:*   Do you need special clothes to do it?
>
> *Leader:*   No, I often TEAPOT in my pajamas.
>
> *Student #4:*   Are there special days or times when you would do this more often than other times?
>
> *Leader:*   I probably TEAPOT more when I daydream.

This continues until a student finds out what the secret word is. Any student can take a guess at the word by raising his hand for the Leader to call on him.

instant artists (3-up)

Cognitive Awareness: making patterns and pictures from half images
Equipment: paper; pencils; magazine pictures; scissors; glue

Procedure: Each student is given a magazine picture that has been cut in half. The object of this activity is for the students to use their imagination to finish the other part of their picture. The students glue the half picture onto the sheet of paper and then draw the other side. If the picture is of half a car, the student must draw what he thinks the other half of the car would look like. Students often have fun trying to draw the other sides of faces and scenes.

   An alternative activity is to give the students pieces of floral-print wallpaper. The students then have to draw what they think would be other parts of the wallpaper print.

a personalized story (3-up)

Cognitive Awareness: language arts
Equipment: pencils; paper

Procedure: Each student thinks up a story about another character who has the same initials as the student. Each student has to weave these initials throughout the story.

   For example: John Smith wants to write a story. His initials are "J" and "S." He thinks of a certain character with the same initials and uses a "J" and the "S" to begin words throughout the story.

THE EXCITING STORY OF JACOB STORMMAKER

   Jacob Stormmaker, the jelly-stomached man, lived in the city of Johnson Stammerville. He would jump stones and fences as he jogged steep hills in the summer days. He had wanted to lose weight in the worst way! One morning he woke up and said to himself: "I know what I can do to lose weight! I will just stop eating so much!"

   He did.

The End

famous folks in history (4-up)

Cognitive Awareness: history facts of famous people
Equipment: slips of paper with the name of a different person written on each one; tape

Procedure: This activity is a good wrap-up event after a history unit that has many famous people in it. Early American history is loaded with famous men and women. Take the slips of paper and tape one to the back of every player.

Each student then walks around the room and talks to the other students as if they were the famous people on their backs.

For example, "George Washington" might hear these comments:

"Well, I see that you are back from the war."

"Good morning, General!"

"Say, where *did* you hide the hatchet?"

"Have you been president long?"

Each student should try to find out as much information as possible about her famous person. When a player correctly guesses who he is, he can take the sheet of paper from his back and tape it to the front of his shirt.

Another way to play this activity is to have the students go around the room asking questions about their famous person. The other students can answer only "yes" or "no" to a student's questions. For example, the player with the name of John Marshall might get the following answers to his questions:

"Was I a president?"	"No"
"Was I a man?"	"Yes"
"Did I have anything to do in the area of law?"	"Yes"
"Was I a chief justice?"	"Yes"
"John Marshall?"	"YES"

yes or no (4-up)

Social Awareness: social interaction
Equipment: five lima beans per student

Procedure: Each student is given five lima beans at the beginning of this activity. During the next ten minutes, each student tries to get other students to either say the word "yes" or "no." If one student gets another to say one of the words then he gets to take one lima bean from that student. The students must talk and answer all questions that are asked of them. Any student who does not answer quickly should be given a penalty and lose a few beans.

You will find that the better students will find ways to answer the questions in other positive or negative words.

The students can roam around the room during this time. All the students should return to their seats after the ten minutes are up.

chapter THREE

ALTERNATIVE
OUTDOOR SPORTS
AND
GAMES

32

Many teachers find it hard to provide activities that can serve as alternative games to the more traditional sports. In the elementary setting, many of the students do not have the skills to successfully play many of the so-called team sports. The games of baseball, football, basketball, and other team sports are often beyond the skill levels of many of the upper elementary children. It is therefore important that other activities be made available to nurture your students' need for exciting and enthusiastic play.

Chapter 3 offers activities that cover a wide spectrum of possibilities. If you teach kindergarten, you will find many of the low organizational activities especially useful. If you teach the intermediate or upper-elementary grades, you will be afforded a refreshing look into other high-interest activities.

firefighter (k)

Cognitive Awareness: auditory recognition of numbers
Equipment: none

Procedure: Make two goal lines about forty feet apart. One student is the Fire Chief and stands about ten feet from the rest of the group. The rest of the class is divided into several small groups. Each group is given a number. The Fire Chief calls out a certain group by saying, "Fire, fire! Station number four!" All the students in station number four run to the opposite goal and back to the Fire Chief. The first person in that group to touch the Fire Chief's hand becomes the new Fire Chief. The game continues with the new Fire Chief calling out for another station. The Fire Chief may call: "General Alarm!" Then all the stations must run. Again the first player to touch the Fire Chief's hand becomes the new Fire Chief.

duck, duck, goose (k)

Cognitive Awareness: readiness for auditory instructions
Equipment: none

Procedure: This is the granddaddy of all low organizational games. All the students sit in a circle. One student is picked as the Duck. The Duck walks around the outside of the circle. She gently touches the head of every student and says "Duck" to every student. When she comes to a person she wants to chase her, the Duck says, "Goose!" as she touches that person's head. The Goose quickly gets up and chases the Duck around the circle. The Duck must try to get back to the vacant spot left by the Goose without being tagged. If the Duck is tagged, the Goose becomes the new Duck. Otherwise, the Duck continues until a new Duck is selected.

word reactions (k-2)

Cognitive Awareness: word-recognition skills
Equipment: one traffic cone

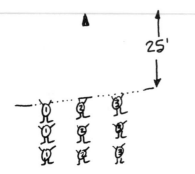

Procedure: The class is divided into two or more groups. Each group is in a file about twenty-five feet from the turning marker. Each player on the teams is given one of the months of the year. When their month is called out, those players must run around the turning marker and back to their place in the line. The first player back will score one point for his team.

This activity can also be used with the days of the week, the alphabet, or numbers.

Another variation on this activity is to have the players who are running step out to the right of their lines as their word is called, run around the turning marker, and re-enter their lines on the left side. This will give your students a little extra practice on learning "left" from "right." It's also a little easier to determine which student came in first when this is done.

imagine (k-2)

Body Awareness: exploring body parts through fantasy
Equipment: none

Procedure: Have the students in a scattered position on the field. The leader will describe how different body parts feel. The other players will have to pretend what the leader is saying. For example:

"Your hands are made of lead."
"Pretend that your body is made of sand."
"Your right hand is a floating balloon."
"Your body is a pool of oil."
"Now your body is on fire."
"Your legs are made of steel."

streets and alleys (k-2)

Cognitive Awareness: following auditory instructions
Equipment: none

Procedure: One person is selected to be the Runner and another person is the Chaser. The rest of the class stand in rows of five or six students each.

Players should be about three feet apart and be able to spread their arms without touching any other player. The players in the rows extend their arms to form passages for the Runner and the Chaser to run in. From time to time, the teacher can signal for the group to change from these streets to alleys. This is done by all the students moving their arms to form passages that are perpendicular to those just made. A simple quarter turn of the body achieves this. Since neither the Runner nor the Chaser can break through the arms of the other students, this changes the direction that the two people must run. The teacher should try and make these signals so as to favor the Chaser. When the Runner is tagged, the Chaser becomes the new Runner. The old Runner returns to the group and another Chaser is selected.

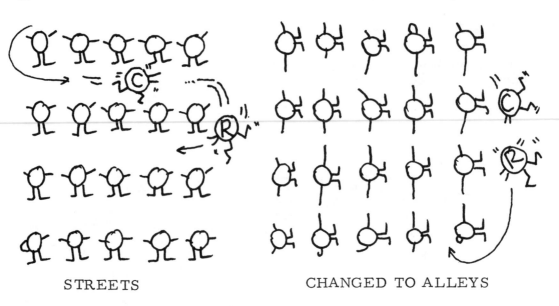

STREETS   CHANGED TO ALLEYS

hook on! (k-2)

Cognitive Awareness: antonym word pairs
Equipment: none

Procedure: This is another pursue tag game. There is one Runner and one Chaser.
The rest of the class stand in a circle facing the center. They form pairs by hooking their
elbows together. Each of these players stands with his outer arms on his hips. This allows
the Runner to hook her arm onto any of the pairs in the circle to avoid being caught by
the Chaser. When this is done, the other partner of that pair must let go and start to run.
That person becomes the new Runner. This allows having many different Runners
during the course of the game. If the Runner is tagged, stop the game and choose two
new people to be the Chaser and Runner.

   After playing this game a few times, you might want to try Antonym Hook On. As
the Runner runs from the Chaser, he shouts "Hot! hot! hot! . . ." as he runs. When he
hooks onto a student pair, the new Runner must shout the antonym to the original
Runner's word before running. The new Runner then shouts a new word as the play
continues.

slowpoke (k-2)

Cognitive Awareness: following commands and recognizing spatial directions
Equipment: none

Procedure: The object of this activity is to follow directions quickly. The class is
divided into pairs. One student is chosen to be the Leader. The pairs must follow the
directions of the Leader.

EXAMPLES

Skip away from your partner.

Touch something blue.

Hop backwards from your partner.

Touch your nose to something hard.

Shake hands with someone wearing boots.

However, whenever the Leader slowly calls out, "Slo-o-ow-po-o-oke!" all students must quickly return to their partners. For example, "Jump to something red . . . touch something green . . . Slowpoke!" You may also want to have the last couples perform a certain stunt. If the Leader calls out the words "Slowpoke" very slowly it encourages the students to try and get back to their partners before the Leader finishes speaking. This is a fun game that can be used indoors and out.

the motorcycle game (k-2)

Body Awareness: exploring personal space
Equipment: none

Procedure: This activity will help your students in distinguishing their own personal space from the space around them. Each student becomes a Motorcycle. They all start off very slowly as they travel in the open areas. Encourage them to try not to bump one another as they do so. As the game progresses, the students can go faster. Whenever the teacher blows a whistle, all Motorcycles must brake to a stop. Any Motorcycle that wrecks with another must go to the garage and sit out the next several Motorcycle runs. This is another good warm-up game for the older students.

germs and the toothbrush (k-2)

Cognitive Awareness: dental health
Equipment: none

Procedure: This activity can be used to reinforce a unit on teeth care. The students are divided into several small groups as shown in the figure above.

Each group should have a Toothbrush and several players who are the Germs. The rest of the students are Teeth. The Germs run around and around the Teeth. The Toothbrush tries to catch the Germs as they run. If a Germ is caught the player becomes another part of the line of Teeth.

The Toothbrush is allowed to run under the arms of the Teeth to catch the Germs. This will help to remind your students that a proper brushing has to take place between the teeth too. Or, if you like, you can assign another student to be the Floss. If this is done, the Floss would naturally be able to go between the teeth to get the Germs.

When all the Germs have been caught by the Toothbrush and the Floss you can start another game by selecting new players to be the Toothbrush, Floss, and Germs.

midnight (k-2)

Cognitive Awareness: telling time
Equipment: none

Procedure: This is a good follow-up activity that contains many of the terms a child would use to tell time. One student is selected to be the Timekeeper. The Timekeeper lives in a small house that is represented by a square drawn on the ground with chalk. This square should be large enough to house several players.

The rest of the class will carefully creep up to the Timekeeper and ask her what time it is. She may answer "Oh, seven-thirty," "Pretty late," "Six o'clock," "Noon," "Time to wake up!" as she continues to let the children get closer and closer.

When the players are close, the Timekeeper says "Midnight!" She then chases the students and tries to tag as many of the players as possible. The students who can get back across the safety line are safe. All the players who have been tagged become helpers of the Timekeeper and stay in the chalk square with the timekeeper until "Midnight!" is called, as the game continues.

When the Timekeeper's house becomes too crowded, you can start the game over.

jack be nimble (k-2)

Body Awareness: running skills
Equipment: none

Procedure: Have your class sitting in a circle. One player is selected to be Jack. He will stand in the center of the circle.

The rest of the class will say the following nursery rhyme:

Jack be nimble,

Jack be quick,

Jack jump over the candlestick!

On the word "candlestick," the player in the center runs and jumps between two of the players in the circle. These two players have to run around the circle in opposite directions. The first player to run and sit down in her original position will be the new Jack.

The game continues with the new Jack running and jumping between two different players.

partner tag (k-2)

Body Awareness: running skills
Equipment: none

Procedure: In this activity, three players are selected to be It. The rest of the players are scattered on the playing field. On a signal the players who are It try to tag as many players as possible. When a student is tagged he is out of the game. The other players can form safety bases by interlocking their arms. Whenever they are in a formation like this the two players are safe and cannot be tagged. However, if two players who are It interlock *their* arms, then they *can* tag the players. This will discourage players from keeping their arms interlocked for long periods of time.

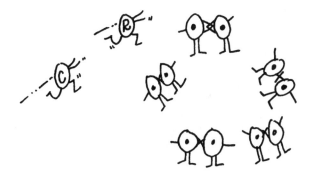

When the majority of players have been tagged you can start over with the selection of three new players to be It.

animal keepers (k-2)

Body Awareness: running and tagging skills
Equipment: none

Procedure: This activity is played using a playground jungle gym. Several players are selected to be the Animal Keepers. The rest of the class scatters out on the playground jungle gym. The Animal Keepers then have to run and tag the other students. If a student is tagged she must go to the jungle-gym cage and wait there until all the children are caught.

When all the students have been tagged you can select other players to be the Animal Keepers and start the game again.

directional beanbags (k-2)

Cognitive Awareness: directional terms
Equipment: beanbags and five hula hoops per group

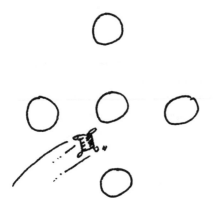

Procedure: The class is divided into several small groups and the hoops are placed as shown. Each group has a Leader who tells the other students where to throw the beanbag. The first player takes three beanbags and throws them at the hoops that are placed about five feet away. The Leader says either "center," "left," "right," "top," or "bottom." The player then has to throw the beanbag at that hoop. He will score one point for every correct throw. The Leader then goes to the back of the line, the Thrower becomes the new Leader, and the player behind him is the new Thrower.

circus tag (k-2)

Body Awareness: identifying body parts
Equipment: none

Procedure: One student is selected to be It. The rest of the class is scattered about the playing area. It is best to play this game without boundaries. On a signal, It tries to tag another student. If another student is tagged, that student must place her hand on the spot where she was tagged. The player who is tagged becomes It. She then tries to tag another student while still holding on to the spot where she was tagged. If a student is tagged on the head, she must place one hand on her head and then try to tag another person. Only one student is allowed to be It at a time. Once another student has been tagged, the old It rejoins the rest of the class.

   The best place to tag another student is on the foot. Then that player has to place one hand on his foot and hop around trying to tag another person.

nose-and-toe tag (k-2)

Body Awareness: being agile and quick
Equipment: none

Procedure: Like the old-time favorite, stoop tag, this game has a position that the players may assume to be safe. But instead of just stooping, each player must kneel down and hook one arm under a leg. At the same time, he must grab his nose with the same hand that is under the leg. He uses this position when he is in danger of being tagged. Before the class plays this game, have everyone try assuming this position. Then pick one student to be It. Have the rest of the class scatter in the playing area and enjoy a good game of Nose-and-Toe Tag.

round 'em up! (k-3)

Body Awareness: running, dodging, and throwing skills
Equipment: four foam-rubber balls

Procedure: Four students are selected to be Cowboys or Cowgirls. These players try to hit the other players with the foam-rubber ball. If a player is hit with the ball he is taken to the cow pen. The cow pen can be any area that the Cowboy selects as long as it is out of the playing area. After all the Cows have been hit each Cowboy or Cowgirl will count up the number of Cows he or she has caught.

   The winner is the player with the most Cows.

   The game continues with the selection of four new Cowboys or Cowgirls.

leaf catching (k-up)

Body Awareness: catching skills
Equipment: a windy autumn day; plenty of leaves

Procedure: This activity is another hard one. Challenge your class to try to catch as many leaves as possible as they drop from the trees. It sounds easy, but it's not! You'll be surprised how hard it is to track a leaf and catch it.

Usually, if a student gets even one leaf she's doing great!

spud (k-up)

Cognitive Awareness: beginning word letters and sounds
Equipment: one utility ball; one base

Procedure: One student starts the game by standing on the base with the ball in his hands. The rest of the players stand nearby in a scattered formation. The Leader throws the ball high overhead and calls out the name of one of the players. All the rest of the players quickly scatter as the player called gets the ball and yells "SPUD!" All players must then stop and stand still—freeze.

The student with the ball names the student she thinks she can hit with the ball and takes three steps toward that player. If the player is hit, he becomes the new Leader as the group returns to the base to start again. If the ball misses the player, the Leader picks a new player to start the game.

Variations: If you are playing this game with older students, you can add some interest by giving the player who was hit by the ball the letter "S." Whenever a student is hit, he is given an additional letter that will spell the word: S-P-U-D. Once a person spells "spud" he is out of the game. In all games of Spud it is wise to have several small groups instead of one large one.

I also use this game to help my students in beginning word letters and sounds. This is done by having the player who catches the ball say the name of the player she intends to hit *plus* the beginning letter and sound of that player's name. This can lead to an exploration of long and short vowel sounds, which can be followed up in classroom instruction.

punctuation dodgeball (k-up)

Cognitive Awareness: language arts
Equipment: one utility ball

Procedure: This activity will help your students in remembering to place a period after each sentence. Multiples of three players in the center of a circle of students are the Sentences. The players in the center form groups of three by holding onto the hips of the person in front of them. The players around the circle will try to "punctuate" each sentence by throwing the ball and hitting the last player in each group. Only the person at the end of each group needs to be hit. If an outside player hits the sentence's tail, then he picks two other players to form another sentence in the circle. The sentence that was hit then becomes a part of the outside group.

A sentence cannot kick the dodgeball away; it can only run and dodge. This is a fun-filled activity, with the sentences trying to keep their tails from being hit.

far base kickball (2-up)

Body Awareness: kicking, rolling, running, and tagging skills
Equipment: one kickball; two bases

Procedure: Place the bases as one would set up a home plate and first base. As in Kickbase (page 74), one team is scattered in the outfield and the other group lines up behind the home plate. The Pitcher rolls the ball to the Kicker. The fielding team can attempt to get the Runner out by tagging her with the ball, tagging the base before the Runner gets there, or by hitting the Runner below the waist. If the Runner is safe, she must wait at first base until the next player makes a fair kick. A fly ball that is caught in the air is out. Three outs and the teams change sides.

Variations:

   1. Use two bases instead of one. This makes the game a little more interesting.

   2. To increase throwing and catching skills, insist that the fielding players have to throw the ball to three different players before trying to get the runner out. If this is done, increase the distance to the base.

butterball (2-up)

Body Awareness: catching and throwing skills
Equipment: four or more foam-rubber balls

Procedure: Divide your class into two groups. Each group is given one side of a basketball court. The center line divides the teams. The students must throw the balls up high in the air toward the opposite group's side. The students on the other side try to catch the balls. Any student who has the ball bounce from his hands to the ground is out and must sit out. This player can return to the game as soon as a player on his team catches a ball. Students who are not paying attention and are hit by a dropping ball must also sit down.

This is a fast-paced activity, since players can be brought back into action *every* time a team member catches a ball. This is a good activity to be played in four three-minute quarters, with the teams switching sides after each three-minute period. Throwing directly at the other team's players is not allowed and should be discouraged.

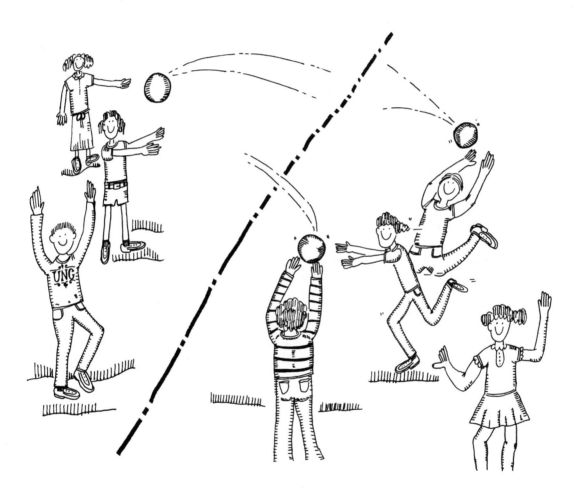

april fools (3-up)

Cognitive Awareness: listening for directions
Equipment: none

Procedure: Have the group stand in a circle with a Leader in the center. The Leader tells the students what to do. For example: "Stand on one foot," "Do five jumping jacks," "Sing like a bird." All the other students must follow the directions of the Leader.

About twenty-five feet away from the circle is a safety line. When the Leader says "April fools!" all the students must run to the safety line without being tagged. If any of the players are tagged they become helpers of the Leader and stand in the center of the circle with her. The fun of the game comes when the Leader gives the group a direction and then quickly says "April fools!"

"Everyone do five jumping—April fools!"

"Stand on one—April fools!"

"Bark like a—April fools!"

Play the game until there are ten players in the center. When the center area becomes too crowded you can select a new Leader and start another game.

mum day (3-up)

Social Interaction: dealing with others
Equipment: one paper flower per student

Procedure: As everyone knows, "April showers bring May flowers." This unique activity uses one of the special May flowers—the chrysanthemum. The object of this activity is to see who can keep "mum" the longest. Give each of your students a small paper chrysanthemum he can tape to his shirt. If a student tricks another into talking to him, the player who talks loses her flower to the student who tricked her.

At the beginning of the activity, with all the students having flowers, it is hard to trick another student without talking. But once a few players lose their flowers, watch out! Since they can talk, they can more easily trick others into talking.

beanbag golf (3-up)

Body Awareness: developing accurate throwing skills
Equipment: several hula hoops; cardboard boxes; #10 tin cans; one beanbag per student

Procedure: The hoops, cans, and boxes are scattered about the playing field at different distances from each other. These objects represent the holes. Each hole should be numbered so that the players will know which hole to go to next. Divide your class into foursomes and assign each group of four to a starting hole. For example, if a group starts off at hole number 5, they will be trying to throw their beanbags into hole number 6 in as few "strokes" as possible. Each player takes his turn in rotation. When the last player gets his beanbag into hole number 6, then the foursome will continue to hole number 7. Each foursome should have a person who acts as the official scorekeeper. The scorekeeper will have a score card with the names of the four players on it. He will be responsible for recording the number of strokes each player took at each hole. Once the players have been at all the holes, each player will add up his score before the official scorekeeper returns the score cards to the teacher.

I have found this activity to be an excellent one for those days when the temperature is too hot for more vigorous games.

rotation basketball (3-up)

Body Awareness: basketball skills
Equipment: one basketball

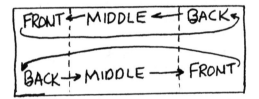

Procedure: Divide the class into teams of nine players apiece. Two teams are then divided evenly in the three sections of the court. Three players from each team are in each of the three sections. Using basketball rules, the game is started by a jump ball in the center by two opposing team members. The object of the game is to pass the ball up to the front players of each team. The three front players try to either make a basket or hit the backboard with the ball. If the backboard is hit, that team scores one point. A basket will score two points.

When the total points of both teams reach a multiple of five, both teams rotate into another section. The back-section players go to the middle, the middle players go to the front, and the front players go to the back area.

For example: The score is 4 to 1. When this happens the teams will rotate into another section. They will play in their new sections until the score reaches a total of ten points.

Remember to stress that only the front players can shoot the ball toward the goal or basket. Once a score occurs, that ball will be put into play by the team that did not score the basket. Play in two fifteen-minute halves.

sock ball (3-up)

Body Awareness: throwing and running skills
Equipment: two bases; one utility ball; one bowling pin

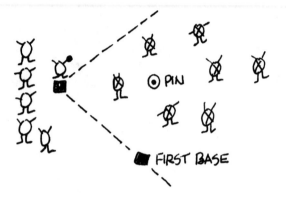

Procedure: The field is formed as shown in the diagram. Use between eight and twelve players per team. The team in the field is scattered about the bowling pin ready to catch or field the ball. The team at home will bat the ball with their fist and run to first base and back home. As soon as the Runner reaches home plate, his team shouts, "Home!" The team in the field tries to retrieve the ball and knock down the pin before the Runner gets home. If the Runner gets home before the pin is knocked down, the runner scores one point.

     The outfield team members cannot run with the ball but must quickly pass the ball from player to player. If the outfield team knocks down the pin before the Runner gets back home, the runner is out. Three outs and the teams change sides. If the outfield team runs with the ball, the Runner automatically scores one point. Any ball that is hit into foul territory is declared an out.

     It saves money over the long run to have the students sock the ball with their fists rather than kicking the ball. A red playground ball doesn't last long if it is kicked!

alphabet soup (3-up)

Cognitive Awareness: language arts
Equipment: two sets of alphabet flash cards

Procedure: Divide the class into two groups. Each player is given a flash card. The players hold the flash cards—face down—on top of their heads. Every player then quickly walks around in a random fashion. The teacher shouts out a certain word. All the players in each team stop and look at their flash card. If their letter is a part of the word, they have to quickly form the word with the other players in their team. The first team to correctly form the spelling word scores one point. This continues with the players walking around the area again. The teacher then calls another spelling word. You may gather up the letters and redistribute them after five words are spelled.

The spelling words must not contain letters that are repeated.

knock down the pin (3-up)

Body Awareness: developing physical fitness
Equipment: one bowling pin per group

Procedure: In this activity, two players will stand on either side of the bowling pin. With the pin between them, the players hold on to each other's hands and try to force the other player to knock down the pin. By pulling and pushing each other, each player tries to get the other to tip over the pin with their feet. The player who knocks over the pin is the loser.

You can divide your class into smaller groups of six to seven players. The first two players will play against each other. The winner of the event will play the next player in line.

crazy olympics (3-up)

Body Awareness: learning track and field events through novelty games
Equipment: paper plates; drinking straws

Procedure: The following events can be held outdoors for your first Crazy Olympics!

Fifty-Foot Dash: The contestants quickly "run" by placing the heel of one foot against the toe of the other. This continues until they reach the finish line.

Discus Throw: Using paper plates for the discus, the players throw the plates for distance.

Javelin Throw: A paper straw is used for the javelin. Each player throws the straw for distance.

400-Meter Relay: Divide your class into groups of four. The first runners on each team have to run around a certain marker and back to their group. When the next player is tagged, he runs around the turning marker and back to the group. This continues until all four players on each team have run. The first team to finish are the winners.

rounders (3-up)

Body Awareness: running, catching, and throwing skills
Equipment: one softball; one bat; set of bases

Procedure: This game dates back to the sixteenth and seventeenth centuries. It was originated in England and is still popular with the children there. While there are many variations of this game, the one presented here is a simple one.

      The game is played on a softball diamond. All the players take positions similar to the game of softball. However, there are a few differences between the games:

    1. The Batter is out if the Catcher is able to catch a fair pitch thrown by the Pitcher. The ball must be a good pitch, not hitting the ground or thrown out of reach of the Batter. Even if the Batter does not swing, he is out if the Catcher is able to catch the pitch. If the ball is hit, any Fielder can catch the fly ball and the Batter is out. As in softball, the Fielders can make an out also by throwing the ball to make a forced out. Tagging the Batter is *not* allowed.

    2. If a Batter makes a safe hit, he is only allowed to advance one base. Therefore, a player making a safe hit advances to first base. If another player makes a safe hit, there would be a player on second base and a player on first base. This type of play continues until a Batter is able to move to home plate. At that time, the Batter scores one point for his team. The fielding team will try to stop this from happening by throwing the ball to a base to cause a forced out. Three outs and the teams change sides.

kickbase (3-up)

Body Awareness: kicking and running skills
Equipment: one kickball; set of bases

Procedure: One team is scattered on the field and the other team is lined up behind the home plate. The Kicker kicks a stationary ball into the playing field and runs the bases. The Kicker scores one point for every base she tags before the fielding team can relay the ball back to the Catcher. The Catcher then places the ball on home plate to stop the play. Every student should be able to have a turn before changing sides.

Variations:

    1. Require the fielding team to stand behind a restraining line until the ball is kicked. This will guard against the occurrence of the fielding players rushing up and quickly getting out a weaker player.

    2. Allowing the fielding players to take only two steps before throwing the ball toward the catcher will encourage the players to pass the ball. Otherwise, the outfielders may attempt to run the ball back to the catcher. By saying that the players must throw the ball after two steps, you increase the chances of more players being involved in the game.

straddle ball (3-up)

Body Awareness: kicking, running, and rolling skills
Equipment: set of bases; one kickball

Procedure: Divide the class into two teams. One team takes the field and the other team kicks. The Kicker is allowed to kick the ball from a stationary position. The fielding team attempts to form a line in the straddle position and roll the ball through the legs of all the players. The end player of the line holds the ball above his head to signal the completion of the task. If the Kicker is able to run all the bases before this happens, she scores one point for her team. If the fielding team performs the task first, no points are scored. Every player is allowed to kick before the teams change places.

Teams preferably should have no more than eight players, but if you decide to use larger numbers of players the distance of the bases can be made longer. Otherwise, the advantage is much in favor of the team kicking the ball.

the great escape! (3-up)

Social Awareness: group problem solving and cooperation
Equipment: one volleyball net; three cardboard boxes; six carpet squares; two long ropes

Procedure: This is an exciting activity for all! The object of the game is for the entire class to successfully travel from a high-voltage electric fence-enclosed area, pass the mine field, through the three manholes, and over the flowing lava to safety. Before the activity begins, inform your class that this is an adventure in class cooperation; everyone has to help out each other person. The class will first be given the problem of getting everyone out of the electric fence (a volley ball net about three feet high). Encourage them to think of ways that would allow everyone to escape. The most frequently used methods include boosting students over or allowing some of the stronger students to be "step stools" as the other students jump carefully from their backs.

If a student touches the fence, he is not eliminated. Just encourage him to try again. Once the entire group is out of the area, they encounter the mine field. At this obstacle the students must jump from the "safe" carpet squares to another safe spot. Have the carpet squares in a zig-zag pattern about three feet apart.

Once through the mine field, the group encounters the guard dogs. Here they must quickly run and hide in the three manholes (three cardboard boxes with the bottom staples removed so that they can crawl through them). One at a time the students run and crawl through the boxes. Space the boxes about ten yards apart. And finally each student must successfully jump over the river of flowing lava. Use two long jump ropes for the lava river. Place the ropes parallel to each other about four feet apart. You may wish to create an extra challenge by forming a lava river that is wider at some points and narrower at other points. This allows the students to pick the portion of the lava flow they wish to jump across.

Once the entire group is across, your class has made a successful escape.

DANGER! LAND MINES

bug catchers (3-up)

Body Awareness: running and tagging skills
Equipment: none

Procedure: The students play on a playing area as shown. Four students are selected to be the Bug Catchers. The Bug Catchers are stationed in each of the four corners of the area. On a signal, they will try to tag as many of the other students as possible. The other students are scattered about the playing area. When a student is tagged by the Bug Catcher she must go and sit down in the Bug Catcher's corner.

Before the game is started, the teacher will secretly pick four Bees. After all the students have been caught by the Bug Catchers, the teacher will tell which students were the secret Bees. The Bees will then go and pretend to sting the Bug Catchers that caught them.

questions, questions (3-up)

Cognitive Awareness: math facts
Equipment: math flash cards

Procedure: This is a tag game that is played with two teams. Divide your class into two groups and have each group line up opposite the other on a basketball midcourt line. The object of this activity is to try to dodge the opponents as one tries to run to the Answer Area. In the Answer Area is an Answer Leader who has a series of math flash cards. A player who safely reaches the Answer Area is shown a flash card. If he answers the question correctly, he receives the card and returns to his starting line to play again. If he answers incorrectly, he returns without the card. If the player is tagged by an opponent before reaching the Answer Area, the runner must return to the midcourt starting line to begin again.

After ten to fifteen minutes, see which team has the most flash cards.

medic (3-up)

Social Awareness:　problem solving and cooperating in groups
Equipment:　two or more foam-rubber balls; two scooter boards (optional)

Procedure:　This game is guaranteed excitement! I still have times when the students will beg to play this game. This is a team dodgeball-type activity. The class is divided into two groups. Each group is given one side of the basketball court as its area. The center-court line divides the teams.

Each team has two Medics who serve as helpers in keeping up their team with healthy players. The object of the game is to try to hit the players on the opposite team. Once a player is hit, she must lie down. The Medics are then responsible for taking the injured player off the playing field to the Hospital. The Hospital can be any area off the playing field. When scooter boards are available, the Medics can transport the injured players to the Hospital with them. Otherwise, they can just hold the player's hand and escort her to the Hospital area.

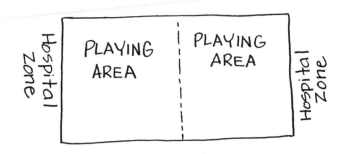

Once in the Hospital, the injured players are allowed to return to their team and start to play again. Balls that are caught can be considered safe.

Other Variations: Another way to play this game is to state that the Medics can be eliminated from the game if they are hit. This will allow a team to possibly win a match by hitting the other team's Medics. Once the Medics are hit, players can no longer be taken to the Hospital and replaced into the game. This means that the other team members must be responsible for seeing that their Medics are protected from being hit. The unselfish action of the team members to block balls should then be encouraged.

It's really wonderful to see the many different ways that the students use to keep their Medics from being hit.

lemonade (3-up)

Social Awareness: pantomiming different activities to the group
Equipment: none

Procedure: Divide your class into two groups. One of the groups thinks up a good activity to pantomime. The two groups meet in the center of the playing area. Behind each group is a safety line about twenty-five feet away.

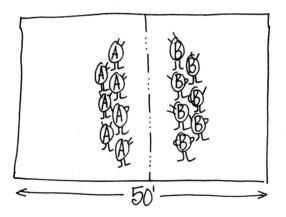

The following dialogue occurs:

Pantomime Group: Here we come.

　　　Other Group: Well, what's your trade?

Pantomime Group: We sell ice cream and lemonade!

　　　Other Group: Then show us some, *if* you're not afraid.

The first group then performs a pantomime activity. The students on the other team try and guess what they are doing. If one of the members correctly guesses what the pantomiming team is doing, the pantomime team runs toward their safety line as the other group chases them. If a player is caught, he will go to the other team. The game continues as the other team thinks of a good activity to pantomime.

　　　PANTOMIME IDEAS
1. Playing football
2. Cleaning up the yard
3. Eating a banana
4. Fishing
5. Tying the shoe of a giant
6. Washing a car
7. Lumberjacks chopping down trees
8. Painting a wall
9. Building a house
10. Cooking a meal

triangle ball (3-up)

Social Awareness: group cooperation
Equipment: three bases; one kickball

Procedure: This activity is a unique kickball game. It centers around team cooperation and full student participation. The bases are arranged to form a large triangle pattern. Using one of the bases as home plate, one team is allowed to kick the ball first. This team has to roll the ball to its own players by providing a Pitcher to do so. Once the ball has been kicked, all the players of the team at bat must form a line and run around the bases. They do this by placing their hands on the shoulders of the person ahead of them. The Kicker is the leader and the Pitcher joins the group as the tail. The team in the outfield must then retrieve the ball. The player who gets the ball first throws the ball to any of her teammates. The goal of the outfield team is to have every member catch the kickball before the home team runs around the bases. After each team member catches the ball, that player tosses the ball to another player and then sits down. If a player misses the catch, he cannot sit down. He can, however, throw the ball to another player. That player can then toss the ball back to him.

If the home team gets every player around the bases before the outfield team finishes catching the ball, one point is scored. No points are scored if the outfield team is able to get every member to catch the ball first.

To help in determining which team finished first, the tail end of the kicking team can shout "Stop!" whenever he touches the home base after running the bases. Another method is to have a student serve as the umpire to determine which team finished first. Each team member should kick the ball. Once this is done, the teams change sides. In this way, there are no outs involved and everyone has a turn to kick. Having six members per team will ensure a fun and interesting game. If there are too many players on the teams, it is harder for the fielding team to stop the home team from scoring.

Variations: This game can also be played by using outs to determine when the teams change sides. If the fielding team finishes before the home team does, an out is the result. All balls that are caught before reaching the ground can also be outs. Three outs and the teams exchange places.

Another way to use this idea is to play a game of Triangle Softball. In this activity, the rules of the game are the same, except that only the Batter runs the bases. For every base the Batter passes before the fielding team finishes one point is scored for the team at bat. If the fielding team finishes before the player runs all the bases, an out is scored. However, that player still gets to count those bases she passed before being out. In this way, even the player who is out can help her team in scoring. Once again, fly balls that are caught are out. Three outs and the teams change positions. Six players per team are ideal.

beat ball (3-up)

Body Awareness: catching and throwing skills
Equipment: two sets of bases; one kickball

Procedure: This is an activity that teaches throwing and catching skills while playing a game. The bases are arranged in the pattern shown above. The inner set of bases are used by the fielding team and the outside set of bases are used by the team kicking the ball. The object of this game is to retrieve the kicked ball and throw it around the inner set of bases before the Kicker runs the outside bases. If the Kicker can get to his home base first, he scores one point for his team. If the fielding team gets the ball passed around from the first baseman and around the bases to home first, then the outfield team scores one point. There are no outs in this game. Either the home team scores a point or the team in the outfield scores one point. This game has one interesting rule: If there is a tie between the runner and the fielding team, award two points to both teams.

The Pitcher also serves as the person who plays home plate for the fielding team. Any ball that is kicked in front of the Kicker's home plate is fair.

This is a very active game. Seven to eight players per team is a good number of players to have. Once every player has a turn to kick, the teams change sides.

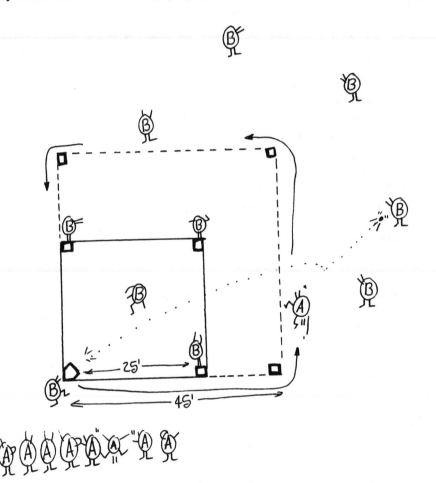

sneakers slap (3-up)

Body Awareness: running skills
Equipment: none

Procedure: The class is divided into two groups. One group lines up about twenty-five feet from the other. One group turns and faces in the opposite direction, each student holding one hand out behind her. On a silent signal, the other team sneaks up to one of the players and slaps her hand. Once a player's hand has been slapped, she turns around and chases the player back to his original line. If the player is caught, one point is scored for the team whose backs were turned.

This is repeated with the other team turned as the opposing team sneaks up on them to slap their hands.

This is done for three rounds. After each round the team points are totaled. The team with the most points are the winners.

soccer keep away (3-up)

Body Awareness: soccer skills
Equipment: one soccer ball per group

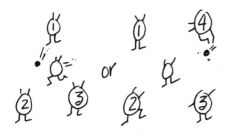

Procedure: Divide your class into groups of four or five players. Each group is given a soccer ball. One player from each group tries to get the ball from the other players in his group. The other players try to keep the ball away from the extra player.

The player in the center changes places when he gets the ball away from the other players. When all the players have had a chance in the center you can start over again.

no fouls, please! (3-up)

Body Awareness: basketball skills
Equipment: one basketball; basketball court

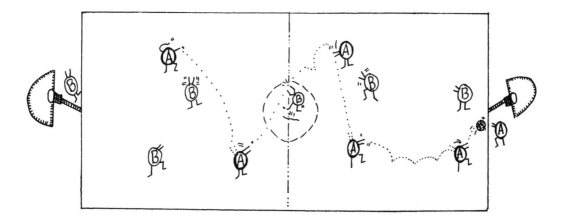

Procedure: I always play this game with my students at the beginning of the basketball unit to help them know what the basic fouls in basketball are. Many of the players turn a game of basketball into a game of tackle football because they do not know what the rules are.

One of the most frequent fouls involves slapping or hitting the arms of the player with the basketball. This is called "hacking." If a student attempts to take the basketball away from another player and slaps the hand or arm of that player, it is a foul. The ball is then taken out of bounds and given to the team of the player who originally had the ball. Now the player who committed the foul is given Strike One. If he commits three fouls he is out of the game.

This activity is played on a basketball court. The object of the game is to try and score points by passing the ball from player to player to the End Player, who stands under a basketball goal. Since the ball may not be dribbled, this game is purely a passing and catching game. If a player takes a full step with the ball, the ball will go to the other team. The player may pivot around one foot, but he is not allowed to take that pivot foot off the ground. If he does, it is called "travelling." This is not a foul but is called a turnover, since the other team gets the ball.

Have about ten players on a team. Select one player from each team to be the End Player. Start game with a jump ball at the center circle. After each score, start the play with a jump ball at the center court circle. Use good judgment to avoid fouls!

five passes (3-up)

Body Awareness: basketball skills
Equipment: one basketball for every ten players; basketball court

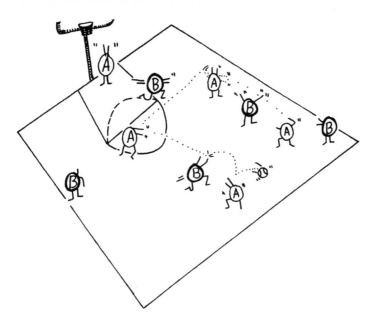

Procedure: The object of the game is to complete five passes. When this is done the team scores one point. There are five players on a team. The game is started with a jump ball at the free-throw line. Using basketball rules, one team tries to have five successful passes. The other team tries to get the ball as it is passed and tries to have five good passes of its own.

    The team with the ball will count aloud for every pass it makes. Five in a row will score one point for the team and the game begins with a jump ball again.

    Play for two ten-minute halves.

3 up/3 down (3-up)

Body Awareness: softball skills
Equipment: set of bases; one bat and one ball for every twelve players

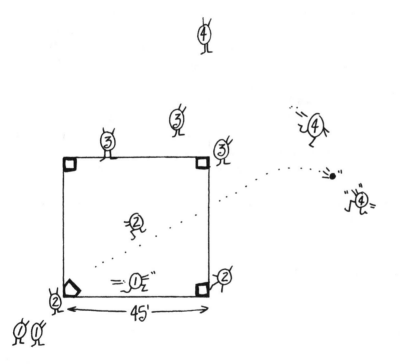

Procedure: Each game is made up of twelve players. These twelve players are divided into four groups of three players each. The object of the game is to see how long one's group of three can stay up at bat. The four groups are given the following positions to start the game:

   1. Three players are at bat first (while the other nine players take their positions on the field).
   2. Catcher, pitcher, first base.

3. Second base, third base, short stop.

4. Left field, center field, right field.

The game is played with softball rules. Once the first three players have made three outs, they move to the outfield positions as the rest of the players rotate forward. Play until each group has had a chance at bat.

kick-off ball (3-up)

Body Awareness: kicking skills
Equipment: one football; one kicking tee

Procedure: This activity is played on a softball field. Divide your class into two teams. One team is out in the field in a scattered formation. The other team lines up behind home plate. Using the kicking tee, or by having another student hold the ball, the first player kicks the football into the field. The fielding team has to retrieve the ball in the following manner: The first player to stop the ball stands with the football above his head. The rest of the players on the team line up behind this player in a single file. The football is then hiked from player to player until it reaches the last player. When the last player receives the ball he holds it above his head as the rest of the students sit down.

While all of this has been going on, the players on the other team have been scoring points. After kicking the football, the first player runs around the line of her teammates. Each time she completes the circle around her group she scores one point. She must stop running as soon as the other team finishes hiking the football to the last player in their line.

Allow five players from a team to kick and run before changing sides. The team that scores the most points after everyone has had a chance to kick will be the winners.

basketball soccer (3-up)

Body Awareness: soccer skills
Equipment: one soccer ball; basketball court

Procedure: This interesting combination of basketball and soccer is played on a basketball court area. Divide the class into two teams. The two teams are further grouped into three smaller squads. One squad from each team is matched against one of the other squads. The other two squads guard the goal line area.

The object of the game is to try to kick the ball across the goal line of the opposite team. If the ball is kicked across the goal line, that team is awarded one point. The squads then rotate, with two new squads given the chance to play.

The main difference from soccer in this game is that if the ball is kicked into the air, the ball may be caught by a player's hands. The player who has the ball may not move from that spot, but can throw it to another teammate. There is then a chance to make a basket to make a score. The ball must be passed from player to player; it cannot be dribbled. If the ball touches the ground, the game will once again resemble its soccer component.

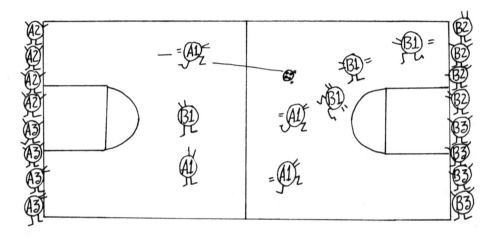

RULES

1. When a ball is kicked across the goal line, it must be no higher than shoulder height. If it is higher, the ball will be given to the opposite team. The goalies are allowed only to trap or block the ball. They may not use their hands.

2. Use basketball or soccer rules whenever possible. Fouls may be treated as in regulation rules.

3. If a basket is scored, it will count for one point. Soccer goals will count as one point.

base tag (3-up)

Body Awareness: dodging and throwing skills
Equipment: ten carpet squares; one utility ball

Procedure: Arrange the carpet squares to form a large circular pattern about twenty-five feet in diameter. The students will stand on one of the carpet squares. Two or more students may need to share a square. One student will stand in the center with the ball. On a signal, the students must run to another carpet square. The player in the center tries to throw the ball at one of the players. If a player is hit, she becomes the new person in the center.

change! (3-up)

Cognitive Awareness: listening for directions
Equipment: one carpet square or beanbag per student

Procedure: Have all the students scatter about the playing area standing on their carpet squares. One student is the Leader. He stands near the center of the playing area. He then calls, "Switch!" All the other students run and get to another carpet square as quickly as possible. The leader also tries to get to a square—only one person to a square. Because the Leader did not have a square, there will be one student who will be without a square. This person then becomes the new Leader. To discourage students from trying to be the Leader, announce that if a student is a Leader for three times he is out of the game. This is a perennial student favorite.

passing challenge (4-up)

Body Awareness: catching and throwing skills
Equipment: one softball per group

Procedure: Divide your class into several small groups, each with seven or eight students. Each group lines up in single file. The first player takes the ball and throws it to the player behind her. The player behind the first player catches the ball and throws it back. The second player then sits down. The first player throws the ball to the third player. The third player catches the ball and throws it back. The third player sits down. This will continue until the first player throws the ball to the last player. The last player catches the ball and passes it back.

 After this short practice all the groups form into one single file. The challenge will be for the class to be able to perform the activity again using all its members. Have the more highly skilled players at the back of the line, as they will have to catch and throw the ball a greater distance. The Leader should be a good catcher and thrower too.

 This is a difficult task. You might want to give your class an extra margin by giving them up to six errors to complete the activity.

blanket volleyball (4-up)

Social Awareness: group cooperation
Equipment: volleyball net; one volleyball; several blankets or towels

Procedure: Each team has twelve players on a team. The object of this cooperative game is to catch the ball in the blanket or towel and throw the ball back over the net. When using blankets, you can have four players holding on to the corners of each blanket. You can use two players when towels are used. It is fun to see if each group can successfully catch the ball in their blanket or towel. Then the players in each group must coordinate their throw by lifting up on the blanket at the same time.

chapter FOUR

All games should be enjoyed by everyone involved. Chapter 4 encourages this by offering you active and fun games that have no losers and eliminate no one during the course of playing. Many of these games and activities are essentially cooperative in nature and allow for positive student experiences that need to happen in your class.

Observations of children engaged in developing and creating their own original games reveal three important points:

1. Children tend to create nonelimination-type activities. They like games that keep everyone involved.

2. Children like to play for fun. Keeping score is usually not as important as we adults seem to think.

3. Children enjoy playing games that have a low frustration level and in which everyone can easily participate. Unlike many of the traditional sports (football, basketball, and baseball) that produce a winner and a loser, child-created games usually need no elaborate system of rules and are simple and easy to play.

So, let's take a hint from the children themselves and play some nongames!

animal chase (k-1)

Cognitive Awareness: naming animals by group
Equipment: none

Procedure: Small children are always interested in animals. Here is a good activity that can help them to remember what to call a group of certain animals.

The Photographer and his Guide stand in the center of the field with the rest of the class behind a starting line. The students are assigned different animal names. There may be a Flock of Birds, a Herd of Elephants, a Gaggle of Geese, a Pride of Lions, or any other animal name that you want to assign to your students. The Photographer and his Guide call out the name of one animal group. The animals in that group must run to a turning point and return to the starting line. The Photographer and his Guide try to tag the animals. Any animal that is tagged becomes a helper. Play continues until all the animals are caught.

bridges and balances (k-1)

Body Awareness: balancing
Equipment: none

Procedure: This is a challenge that you can use with your students. Give them the following challenges:

1. Can you make a bridge using four body parts? Using three body parts? Using two feet and two hands? Two hands and one foot?
2. Can you balance on two body parts? Can you balance on one body part? On another body part? On one knee?
3. Can you make a bridge with four body parts and your back to the ground? Can you make a bridge with two feet and one head? Can you make a bridge with one hand and one foot?
4. Can you balance on three body parts? Can you balance on your hands? On your head and hands? On one hand?

Try adding other challenges to this list.

fox in the morning (k-2)

Body Awareness: practicing different ways to move
Equipment: none

Procedure: The class stands in a line about twenty feet from the Fox. The object of this activity is to try to run across the playing area and get to the other side without being tagged by the Fox. Before the players can run, the Fox will ask them to perform certain skills.

Players: Fox in the morning, Fox at night,
Can we run with all our might?

Fox: Yes, you may, yes, you might,
If you can do a *cartwheel* tonight!

The students who can do a cartwheel will do one and then run across. If the Fox catches a student, he becomes her helper as the Fox continues to ask the rest of the class different physical skills to perform.

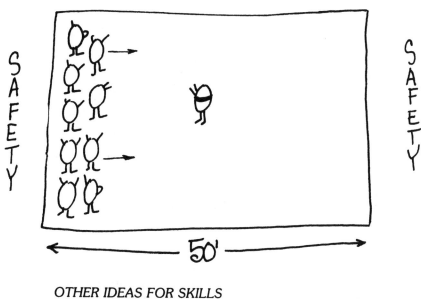

OTHER IDEAS FOR SKILLS

1. Jump and turn around
2. Twist and turn
3. Act like a monkey
4. Walk on your hands
5. Stand on one foot
6. Sing like a bird
7. Do a back bend
8. Shake hands with a friend

The game continues until the last player is tagged.

flowers and the wind (k-2)

Cognitive Awareness: identifying flower names
Equipment: none

Procedure: The class is divided into two teams, the Flowers and the Wind. The groups line up facing each other. The Flowers are given the name of a flower by the teacher. The Flowers then walk up to the other players. When they are about five feet away, the Wind players try to guess what flower all the Flowers are. If the correct answer is given, the Flowers run back to their safety line. If a Wind player tags a Flower, then that player is out. The roles are reversed as the new Flower group is given the name of a flower.

Different clues can be given the guessing team if they are having a difficult time in guessing the name of the flower. For example, if the flower name was buttercups, a clue could be "This flower goes well with bread," or "This flower tastes good."

mr. spider's paint store (k-2)

Cognitive Awareness: using deductive logic from a series of hints
Equipment: none

Procedure: This is a wonderful game of make-believe and imagination. Mr. Spider stands in front of the rest of the class. The students should be in a line about ten feet from Mr. Spider's paint store. Mr. Spider asks one of the student Flies what color paint she wants to buy. "Miss Tracy Fly," asks Mr. Spider, "what color paint would you like to buy?" "Red," replies Miss Tracy Fly. Mr. Spider then goes and gets a make-believe can of

paint, shakes it up, takes the lid off, and looks in the can. If "red" was the color Mr. Spider was thinking of, Mr. Spider says, "Yes, I have red!" The students then run to the safety line. If Mr. Spider tags one of the Flies, he becomes one of Mr. Spider's helpers. The untagged Flies then return to the starting line. Mr. Spider tells his new helpers another secret color and the game continues.

This an excellent game to play at the beginning of the year. I usually enjoy being Mr. Spider because it helps me to remember the names of the students. I do this by introducing my new helpers to the class after each round. Clues can also be given if the colors are more difficult. "This color begins with the letter B," or "The color is a cold color."

the bridge (k-2)

Cognitive Awareness: recognizing colors
Equipment: none

Procedure: Mark off a bridge—two parallel lines about ten feet apart—in the middle of the playing area. The Bridgekeeper stands on the bridge and tries to tag the players as they cross from one side of the playing area to the other. Any player who is tagged becomes a helper of the Bridgekeeper and can try to tag other players who cross the bridge. To start the game, all the students stand on one side of the playing area as the Bridgekeeper calls out a certain color. All those players who are wearing the color have to run to the other side. If they reach the other side safely, they stay there. The Bridgekeeper continues to call out colors until all the players get the chance to cross.

The game continues with the Bridgekeeper turning to face the "safe" players on the other side and calling out other colors so that they try to run to the opposite side. When the bridge becomes too crowded, pick another Bridgekeeper and start the game over again.

Besides calling out certain colors, the Bridgekeeper can ask:

"If you can do a cartwheel . . . come over!"

"All those people with younger sisters . . . come over!"

"If you like pizza . . . come over!"

run, rabbit, run (k-2)

Cognitive Awareness: following directions
Equipment: none

Procedure: This is an old favorite. One student is the Hunter. The Hunter stands facing the rest of the class, who are in a line about ten feet away. The Hunter points to a distant object—a fence, pole, or tree—and calls, "Run, rabbits, run!" The class runs to that object. The Hunter tries to tag as many of the Rabbits as possible. Any students who are tagged become helpers of the Hunter. The game continues as the Hunter calls out another object. The Hunter and his helpers try to tag the running Rabbits. The game starts over when all the Rabbits are caught.

cranes and crows (k-2)

Cognitive Awareness: distinguishing *a* and *o* sounds
Equipment: none

Procedure: This game is best played on a basketball court because of its boundaries. The class is divided into two groups: the Cranes and the Crows.

The Cranes and the Crows line up facing each other about ten feet apart along the midcourt line. A Leader then calls out either "Cranes" or "Crows." If the Leader calls "Crows", then the Crows will turn and run to the goal line behind them. The Cranes will attempt to tag as many of the Crows as they can before they reach the goal line. Any Crow who is tagged becomes a member of the Cranes group and lines up on their line. The game continues as both groups reassemble at the center court area. When the leader calls "Cranes" the Cranes have to run to the goal line behind them. If any of the Cranes are tagged by the Crows, they become members of the Crows group. This game aids in building your students' listening skills, as they have to distinguish the different letter sounds.

circle sounds (k-2)

Cognitive Awareness: rhyming sounds
Equipment: none

Procedure: Have your class form a large circle. Go around the circle and assign your students numbers by counting off by fours. Then recheck to see if every student remembers his number. I am always surprised at the many students who have trouble remembering their numbers. The object of this game is for the students to run around the outside of the circle whenever they hear a word that sounds like their number. They return to their original place after running around the circle one time. Practice with your students by giving them example words before starting the game.

> *One:* Fun, bun, run, sun
>
> *Two:* New, shoe, glue, blue
>
> *Three:* Knee, me, bee, see, flea
>
> *Four:* Door, sore, more, roar

You can call out a rhyming word for the students to run to. As soon as one group finishes, call out another rhyming word.

cross the brook (k-2)

Body Awareness: jumping and landing skills
Equipment: two ropes

Procedure: The ropes are placed parallel to each other about three feet apart. The class jumps over the ropes one at a time. The ropes represent the two banks of a river. The students should jump over the ropes and land correctly. When the students land, they should "give" with their legs to cushion their landing. The two ropes can be made wider apart as the game continues. If a child doesn't make it across the creek, she should pretend she has fallen in the water and gotten wet. This activity is a favorite of younger children. Another way to vary the challenge of the activity is to have the far rope in a sideways "S" shape. This allows the choice of either jumping across the wide part or the near part of the far rope.

superman (k-3)

Body Awareness: running and tagging skills
Equipment: none

Procedure: Four students are selected to be the Leaders. The Leaders try to tag the other players. When a student has been tagged, he must freeze, put his hands on his hips, and spread his feet apart. He can reenter the game if another student crawls under his legs.

While this game can be played with a large group, you might want to divide your class into smaller groups and play several games at the same time. When the number of players is smaller (five to eight players) you can have one player be the Leader. A student who has been tagged three times becomes the new Leader.

This novel freeze-tag activity will soon become one of the popular games on the playground.

nonelimination musical chairs (k-3)

Social Awareness: cooperating in a group
Equipment: record player; records

Procedure: Here is a new twist on an old classroom delight—musical chairs. It is played like regular musical chairs with this slight modification: instead of the elimination of players, the students must cooperate and share the available chairs to accommodate all the members of the class. As each chair is removed, the players must either sit on one another's laps or share chairs. It's an interesting activity both to be in and to watch.

circle seat (k-3)

Social Awareness: cooperating in a group
Equipment: none

Procedure: Have you ever tried to sit down without a chair? Do you believe that your whole class can sit down without using any chairs at all? It's simple. Arrange your class into a circle formation. The students should be about six inches away from each other, facing in a clockwise direction. On a given signal, each child *slowly* sits down on the knees of the person behind him. This is best done by having each student hold the hips of the person in front of him and guiding the player's hips to his knees. If all goes well, you will end up with one large circle of seated players.

nature walk (k-3)

Social Awareness: role playing and self-expression
Equipment: none

Procedure: This activity is one for a nice spring day. Take your students outside for a nature walk. As you walk, pretend and role play the following situations:

> Smelling a pretty flower
> Picking wild berries
> Being stung by a bee
> Feeding some ducks
> Backing into a thorny bush
> Jumping over a small log
> Looking for a bear
> Being hit on the head by an acorn
> Swimming across a lake
> Doing cartwheels across a daisy field
> Running through cornstalks
> Starting a campfire
> Drinking water from a well

statue makers (k-up)

Social Awareness: cooperating and trusting in a group
Equipment: none

Procedure: Divide your class into groups of three. Each group has this scene described to them.

> One player in each of the groups has to pretend that he is a big block of marble. Now the other two players are the statue makers. They will pretend to use their hammers and chisels to form a beautiful sculpture out of the piece of marble that is lying on the ground. Once the sculpture is finished, the two statue makers will have to lift the statue up to show it to the rest of the class.

The students then pretend to chip away their beautiful masterpiece that lies in the marble. When they are finished, they have to lift the marble figure to its feet. The student who is the statue has to tense up his body so that he is strong and solid like marble. The two statue makers then show their latest project. Allow enough time for each of the three players to be the block of marble and the newly revealed statue.

A good group will cooperate in every way. Encourage the statues to be stiff and strong. As the other two players lift the statue up, the statue should remain "as solid as marble."

sailors and sharks (3-up)

Body Awareness: exploring dynamic force and one's center of gravity
Equipment: none

Procedure: Here is a simple activity that can be used as a warm-up game. Using a 16-foot-diameter dodgeball circle, the fun begins.

"This area is the boat," you say, pointing at the circle. "It is surrounded by sharks. The sharks try and pull the sailors into the 'sea' and the sailors try to pull the sharks into the boat. If you are pulled on the boat, you become a sailor. If you are pulled off the boat you change from a sailor to a shark."

Divide the class into Sailors and Sharks and go.

Of course, any number of playground markings can be used for the boat. There are no rules against a square-shaped boat. Use whatever you can find. I have used colored chalk and let my students draw their own boats.

You can increase your students' awareness of their centers of gravity (usually about their hips) by telling them that an object with a low center of gravity is more stable than one with a high one. They will easily see this in action as they find themselves crouching down to prevent being pulled over.

nonelimination dodgeball (3-up)

Cognitive Awareness: spelling words
Equipment: set of alphabet flash cards; a list of spelling words

Procedure: This game is played like the traditional dodgeball game, except that whenever a player is hit, she has the opportunity to get back into the game by performing a certain stunt.

   For example, one student has just been hit by the ball. Ordinarily, she would either become one of the throwers or just sit out. Instead, she has to arrange a set of letter cards to form one of her spelling words or put the letters in alphabetical order or perform any other task, such as:

   Do five jumping jacks.

   Do a back bend.

   Make a bridge using two hands and one foot.

Another interesting idea is to use couple stunts. Whenever a student is hit, he must wait until another player is hit. These two players then perform a couple stunt such as the following to get back into the game.

Wring the Dishrag: This stunt is performed by having both students hold hands above their heads and twist around without breaking their grasp.

Back-to-Back Getup: This stunt is performed by having the students sit back to back on the ground. They interlock elbows and attempt to stand up together.

santa and the elves (3-up)

Body Awareness: throwing skills
Equipment: two or three foam-rubber balls

Procedure: This activity is played using a circular pattern as the playing area. Many schools have these markings for dodgeball playing areas. Draw a smaller circle about ten feet in diameter in the center of the larger circle.

One student is selected to be Santa. He stands in the center of the smaller circle. Also pick three Elves to be his helpers. The Elves stand on the smaller circle. The rest of the class is scattered about the larger circle. They try and throw the foam-rubber balls at Santa. The Elves have the job of trying to protect Santa from being hit. They use their arms to knock down the balls as they come. The outside players can retrieve a ball that is knocked down by one of the Elves, but they can only throw at Santa if they are behind the larger circle.

When Santa is hit, the player who hit him becomes the new Santa. The teacher can pick three new Elves.

Since Santa cannot move from the center of the small circle to dodge a ball, it is essential that the three Elves work together to protect Santa from the balls.

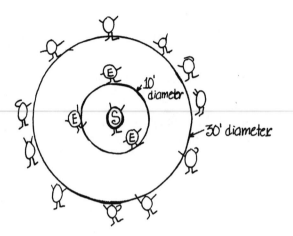

back-to-back tag (3-up)

Body Awareness: running and tagging skills
Equipment: none

Procedure: In this tag game the students are safe whenever they stand back to back with another player. Select several players to be It. If a player is tagged by a student who is It, the player who was tagged becomes the new It.

To keep from having too many of the students just standing back to back throughout the activity, a special player called the Crowbar may be called to "split" a pair of students apart. The Crowbar and the players who are It work together as a team. When two players who are back to back are touched by the Crowbar, the two players must run apart from each other.

While the players who are It may change during the course of the game, the player who is the Crowbar will remain the same player throughout the entire game. You may want to stop the game and select another student to be a new Crowbar if the old one seems to be a bit too tired.

the two-headed monster (3-up)

Body Awareness: running and tagging skills
Equipment: none

Procedure: This activity can take place on a basketball court or any other suitable playing area. The game starts off with the two players who are the Monsters in the center of the playing area. The rest of the class lines up on one side of the court. The two players in the center interlock their arms and slowly turn around as they chant:

> *A two-headed monster we be,*
>
> *We'll chase you, one . . . two . . . three!*

When the players say "three!" the students who are on the sidelines run and try to make it to the other side without being tagged by one of the students in the center. The Two-Headed Monster then unlocks the four arms and runs to tag the students. If any of the students are tagged they become the new helpers of the Monster.

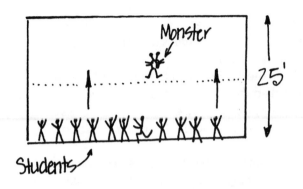

For example, if three players were tagged before reaching the other side safely, these three players would interlock their arms with the original two students and say:

> A *five-headed monster we be,*
>
> *We'll chase you, one . . . two . . . three!*

The students would then unlock their arms and try to chase the other players as they run back toward the other side. All students tagged become helpers.

it's a tie! (3-up)

Social Awareness: cooperating in a group
Equipment: none

Procedure: This is an activity that depends on the total cooperation of the entire class to work. Each student is paired with another student. The two students run to a given finish line and attempt to end up in a tie. Then each pair is matched up with another couple and the four of them attempt to finish in a tie. This process continues until the entire class forms one giant race with everyone ending up a winner!

everyone's it tag (3-up)

Body Awareness: changing speeds and directions in space
Equipment: none

Procedure: Here is nonstop activity in action! Using given boundaries (a basketball court, for example), every student is It. If a student tags another student, the tagged player must sit down. If two players tag each other at the same time, both players must sit down. This activity has instant student participation and appeal because of its easy rules. The game continues until there is only one student left. You can also add more player participation by allowing the seated players to tag the runners as they pass by. This causes the players to be on the watch for both the running players and the seated players.

octopus (3-up)

Body Awareness: changing speeds and directions in space
Equipment: none

Procedure: Play this activity on a basketball court area. Have the class line up along the long side of the court. One student is the Octopus and stands in the center of the court. The Octopus calls out "Fishes come on!" The students run across the court and try to get to the other side without being tagged by the Octopus. If they are tagged by the Octopus, the players must kneel on one knee where they were tagged. They can wave their arms and try to tag other students who may be "swimming" by. The kneeling students cannot move from their spots. The game continues with the Octopus turning to face the rest of the players on the other side line and saying "Fishes come on!" For more fast-paced action, have more than one Octopus.

playground computer (3-up)

Cognitive Awareness: math facts
Equipment: math flash cards; computer diagram

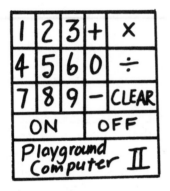

Procedure: Draw the computer diagram on a playground blacktop surface. The squares should be big enough for a student's foot to fit in easily. The object of this game is to jump from one space to the other as requested by the player who has the math flash cards. For example, if the leader has the flash card 5 × 8 = ? the student has to do the following things:

1. He jumps onto the "on" square . . .
2. From the "on" square he jumps to the "5" square . . .
3. Then to the "×" square . . .
4. Then to the "8" square . . .
5. Then to the "=" sign.

The player then has to figure out the answer to the flash card and jump to the answer. Since the answer of 5 × 8 is 40, the student jumps to the 4 and the 0 squares.

6. After jumping to the number 40, he jumps to the "off" square.

If a player makes a mistake he can jump to the "clear" square and start again. The student may not land on a line.

In addition, you could have other types of playground figures drawn permanently on the blacktop area. Besides the computer figures, many schools have a large picture of the United States outlined on their playing area.

What a wonderful way to study geography!

greek dodgeball (3-up)

Body Awareness: throwing, dodging, and catching skills
Equipment: two or three utility balls

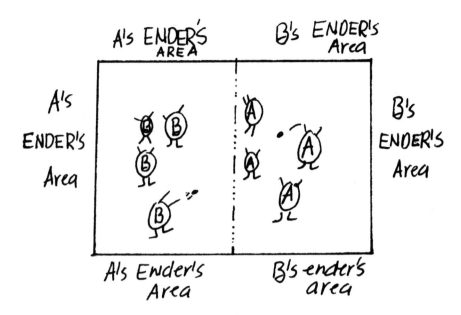

Procedure: This is a great way to play dodgeball so that no one is eliminated from playing. Divide your class into two teams. Using the boundaries of a basketball court, each team lines up on its side of the basketball court. The object of the game is to be the first team to get the other players out by hitting them below the waist. Each player who is hit becomes an Ender and moves to one of the three sides that surround the other team. The Enders can throw the ball back and try to hit an opponent below the waist. If an opponent catches the ball the player who threw the ball is out. The ball has to be caught while it is still in the air before it has landed.

As a team has more of its members out of the court area, it will have more players in its Enders area and can surround the opponents with players who will try to get them out.

Give each team a ball to start the game. The first team to get all of its opponents out is the winner.

You might want to use foam-rubber balls to play this game. These balls are softer and your students are less likely to get hurt when they play. You may also want to have a few of the players on each team start the game as Enders.

trust fall (3-up)

Social Awareness: cooperating and trusting in a group
Equipment: none

Procedure: You begin this activity by having the students form groups of three players. One player has to stand about two feet in front of the others and fall backward toward her partners. The partners allow the player to fall a short distance and then push the player back up to her original position.

The object of the activity is for each group to have a good experience in forming a sense of trust in the others as they catch the falling player and allow her to feel the act of falling in a safe and enjoyable manner.

The player who is falling should keep her body tight and straight. The arms should be at her side as she slowly falls backwards. The two other players should contact the player with their hands almost as soon as she starts to fall. They will slow down her fall and push her back up to her starting position. As the two players become more confident of their catching abilities, they can allow the falling player to fall for a longer distance. Continue this until each member of the group has had at least one turn to fall.

There will be a few students who may not want to try falling backwards. Try to encourage these students to give it a chance. They usually find it so much fun that they're the first to ask if they can do it again.

If there are a few groups that are very good at this activity, you might challenge them to try a trust rocker. A trust rocker is done by having one player standing between two side players. The player in the center falls from side to side as the two outside students catch the center student and push him back toward the center again. The two side players should start the activity by being very close to the middle player. As they become more comfortable with their abilities they can catch the center player from a longer distance.

the tape game (4-up)

Social Awareness: social interacting
Equipment: a roll of masking tape

Procedure: This activity is a great one for developing a sense of group problem ownership and problem solving. Divide your class into about five smaller groups of players. Each group will be given the task of placing a piece of masking tape as high as they can up the side of an outside wall.

One at a time each group will be given five minutes to talk about the most effective way to place the tape as high as possible. This may mean having some players stand on the backs of others, having some players boost lighter players up the wall, or whatever methods the group wishes to explore. During this five-minute period they must decide on a way to place the tape the highest on the wall.

After all the groups have had a chance to place their tape on the wall, the group with the highest tape is the winner.

Follow up this activity with a group discussion on the various ways that were used to accomplish their goal. Why did certain ones work best? Not so well?

You can also award extra points to the teams that use all their students in the formation used to place the tape on the wall.

unvolleyball (4-up)

Body Awareness: volleyball skills
Equipment: volleyball net; one volleyball

Procedure: This activity is played as a regular game of volleyball with the following exception:

When a player hits the ball over the net, he runs under the net and becomes a member of the other team.

This activity is a sharing experience. The object of the game is to see if all the players on both teams can exchange places. All the other members try to help their teammates hit the ball over the net.

If everything goes well, all the players will have switched sides when the volleyball game is over.

chapter FIVE

FOR THE CLASSROOM

RELAYS

AND FOR OUTDOORS

This chapter offers nonstop relay fun. Many of the relays are geared to enhance class participation, enjoyment, and interaction. Unlike most relays, however, these cooperative relays downplay competition. You should make sure that positive and affirming interactions happen between students during a physical education period. Using Chapter 4's relays will help you do that.

While these relays can serve as warm-up activities, you can also use them as teaching tools to help with movement skills. Younger children can reinforce their throwing, catching, and balancing skills by incorporating them into a relay event. Your older students will enjoy learning sport skills through this relay format. In fact, it is much easier to present team sport skills (throwing a football, passing a basketball, and bunting a softball) via relays than any other method.

Encourage the teams to try and do a certain relay under a set time limit. This encourages everyone to do his or her best without the stress of having to win or lose. By having a time limit to compete against, the teams are not pitted against each other. Of course, the time limit should be both challenging and flexible so that every team can be successful.

shirt-button relay (k)

Body Awareness: fine motor coordination
Equipment: one old shirt per team

Procedure: Divide the class into two or more teams. Place the shirts, unbuttoned, directly across from each team on the other side of the room. The first player on each team has to run to the shirt and button one of the buttons. This player runs back to his team and tags the next player. The next player runs up to the shirt and buttons another button. This continues until all the buttons on the shirt are buttoned.

The first team to button all the buttons on its shirt is the winner. Since there are usually only five or six buttons on a shirt, unbutton the shirt and play another relay so that all members of the class get to play. Always have shirts that have the same number of buttons for each team.

sore-toe relay (k)

Body Awareness: identifying body parts
Equipment: none

Procedure: Divide your class into two teams or more. Have each team line up in a single file behind a starting line. The first player has to hold her left foot with her right hand as she walks to the turning point and back to her group.

The rest of the players continue in the same fashion. Have the students hold different body parts as they run other relays in the same manner.

alphabet relay (k-1)

Cognitive Awareness: learning the alphabet
Equipment: alphabet flash cards for each team

Procedure: Divide the class into two or more teams. Place a set of shuffled alphabet flash cards in a pile in front of each team. The cards should be face up about fifteen feet from the starting line. On signal, the first player runs to his pile of cards and finds the letter "A." The player places the card above the pile. He then runs back to the group and tags the next player. This player runs to the pile and finds the letter "B" and places it next to the letter "A." This continues with each player placing the next letter in correct order. The first team to finish the alphabet is the winner.

peanut-passing relay (k-1)

Body Awareness: passing objects in a cupped hand
Equipment: ten peanuts per team

Procedure: Divide the class into two or more teams. The students in each team line up their seats in a row. The ten objects are placed in front of the first players of each team. On a signal, the first player picks up one of the objects and places it in her cupped hand. She proceeds to pass the object to the player at her side. Each player has to use a cupped hand to receive and pass the object. When the object gets to the last player, he will place the object in a pile near his seat. Then the last player runs to the front of the team and places another object in the cupped hand of the leader. This object is then passed back again to the last player. The first team to get all ten objects to the end of their line should wait quietly for the rest of the class to finish.

over/under relay (k-1)

Cognitive Awareness: learning spatial terms *over* and *under*
Equipment: one ball per team

Procedure: Divide your class into two or more teams. Have each team line up in a single file with the students' legs apart. On a signal, the first player takes the ball and lifts it up and over his head with his two hands. The player behind him takes the ball and brings it under his legs. The next player grabs the ball and lifts the ball up and over his head. The ball continues to go over and under all the players until it reaches the last player. The last player then runs with the ball to the front of the line and passes the ball over her head to the next player.
      When the original leader gets to the front of the group again, the team quickly sits down.

partner-pair relay (k-1)

Body Awareness: using different locomotor skills
Equipment: none

Procedure: In this relay have your students hold hands in pairs.
      Certain locomotor movements have to be performed. First, have the pairs run to a certain point. Skipping, hopping, leaping movements can also be used in this relay. Divide your class into smaller groups and have a partner pair relay race.

shoe-pile relay (k-2)

Body Awareness: fine motor coordination
Equipment: none

Procedure: Divide your class into two or more groups. The groups line up behind a starting line. Have each member of the class take off her right shoe. Each shoe is taken and placed in a pile on the other side of the room. All shoes must be untied. On a signal, the first player on each team runs to the shoe pile and finds her shoe. The player must then put her shoe on and tie it. After the shoe is tied, the player can run back to her team and tag the second player. The first team to finish the relay is the winner. It is a good idea to have either the teacher or another student as the shoe-tying judge to make sure the shoes are correctly tied before the player runs back to his group.

Variations: After you have finished playing the Shoe Pile Relay, you might want to try another similar relay. Instead of using shoes, you can try a Belt-Tying Relay. In this relay, have all the students who are wearing belts participate. This activity will have the students running to a pile of belts and putting them on. Once the belt has been correctly put on, the player runs back to his team. The team that finishes first is the winner.

animal-walk relay (k-2)

Body Awareness: moving in different ways
Equipment: none

Procedure: Divide the class into two or more groups. On a signal, the first players move from the starting line to a designated turning point and back. Each of the players has to imitate a certain animal walk. You can pick from the following styles:

1. *The bear walk.* The bear walk is performed with the player on all fours. Instead of crawling in the normal manner of using opposite arms and legs, the student must move using the same leg and hand. For example, the student must move his left arm and left leg, then his right arm and right leg to crawl. The usual crawling pattern would be to use the left hand with the right leg and the right hand with the left leg. In fact, the occurrence of this nonoppositional pattern of crawling in older students may indicate an immature movement problem.

2. *The seal walk.* The seal walk is performed by using the arms to drag the rest of the body. The student keeps her legs together and shuffles her hands to drag her legs from side to side. Some of my students call this a "walking push-up," since it is similar to a push-up position.

3. *The crab walk.* The crab walk is performed by sitting down on the floor and using the hands and feet to move. By lifting the body, the student can easily move by shuffling his feet and hands.

4. *The kangaroo walk.* This is performed by having the student hop across the room and back with his hands held in front of him.

5. *The horse walk.* The horse walk is just a gallop movement. A gallop is performed by keeping one leg in front of the other and quickly shuffling the feet.

puzzle race (k-2)

Cognitive Awareness: visual memory and visual spatial skills
Equipment: several puzzles of twelve or more pieces

Procedure: Divide your class into as many groups as you have puzzles. Four groups are the best. The first player has to run to the puzzle in front of his group and put two pieces together. He then runs back to his group. The next player runs to the puzzle and puts two pieces together. This continues until the puzzle is complete.

goat-butt relay (k-2)

Body Awareness: butting a ball
Equipment: one utility ball per group

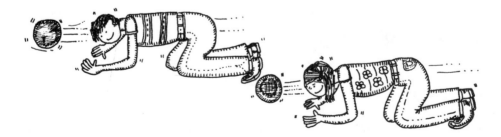

Procedure:　This activity is done by having the students butt a ball to a turning line and back again. The first player gets on her hands and knees and starts to butt the ball with her head. Play continues until every student has had a turn. Divide your class into smaller groups and play. It's a game where they *really* have to use their heads!

chariot relay (k-2)

Social Awareness:　cooperating and sharing
Equipment:　none

Procedure:　This relay takes the combined efforts of three people as a group. Two players hold their inside hands together. The third player stands behind the two and grabs hold of their outside hands. This forms one chariot.
　　　　Divide your class into two or more teams and have a chariot race.

tunnel-ball relay (k-2)

Social Awareness:　cooperating on a given task
Equipment:　one ball per team

Procedure:　Have each team line up with their legs spread apart in the straddle position. The first player passes the ball under his legs to the last player in line. The last player gets the ball and runs to the front of the group. She then straddles her legs and rolls the ball under all the legs of the group to the last player. When the first player to roll the ball is in the front of the group again, all the team members sit down.

movement-challenge relay (k-3)

Cognitive Awareness:　using symbols for movement patterns
Equipment:　one set of flash cards with the numbers 1 through 5 each on a different card

Procedure:　This is a simple relay event. After dividing your class into relay teams, explain to them that they will be using different locomotor movements for this relay. The Leader stands in front of the group and shows one of the flash cards. Each of the numbers will represent a different way to move from the starting line to the turning point and back.

1. Means to skip
2. Means to walk backwards
3. Means to hop on one foot
4. Means to run
5. Means to jump with two feet

Each player must look to the Leader for the correct way to move before he starts. It would be a good idea to spend a few minutes in practicing what the numbers mean before the relay is performed.

More challenging movements should be given to the older students. These may include doing jumping jacks moving forward, skipping backwards, the grapevine step, a side shuffle, and doing cartwheels.

apple-tart relay (k-3)

Social Awareness: cooperating in a group
Equipment: one beanbag per team

Procedure: Divide the class into two teams. Have each team stand in a single file. The last player in line is given a beanbag. On a signal, this player runs to the front of the line and gives the Apple Tart (beanbag) to the first player. The Apple Tart is then passed down the line to the end player. The end player runs to the beginning of the line and passes the Apple Tart again. When the original last player gets to the end of the line again, her team sits down. The first team to finish should quietly wait until the rest of the class is finished.

cross-over relay (k-3)

Social Awareness: cooperating and sharing in a group
Equipment: none

Procedure: Divide your class into four teams or more. The teams line up in a single file behind a restraining line. The Leader stands in front of his team behind another line about twenty-five feet away. On a signal, the Leader runs to the first player in his team. He grabs that player's hand and both run back to the other line. The Leader leaves the player at this line and goes back for another player. When all the Leader's teammates are across, that group has to sit down in line.

Because the Leader has to run the whole time, it is wise to have no more than six players per group.

Another way to play this game is to allow the Leader to run and grab the first player. They both run back to the other line, *except* it is the Leader who stays there. The other player then runs to the line and grabs a second player. The first player is left at the other line as the second player runs to get another teammate. In this way, no one person has to run during the entire relay.

cup-blow relay (k-up)

Social Awareness: group cooperation
Equipment: two paper cups; pencil; string

Procedure: Using a pencil, poke a hole in each of the paper cup bottoms. Then place each cup on a string that is supported between two chairs or other objects. Each player tries to blow the cup from the starting line to a designated finish point. The same player carries the paper cup back to the starting line for the next player to blow. Divide your class into teams and let the fun begin. Do not have the string over fifteen feet long because many of your students will hyperventilate during this activity if the distance is too long. This activity can also be used as an academic tie-in during study of the respiratory system.

Variations: Another way to play this game is to blindfold your students and have them try to blow the cup along the string. The other members in line will be able to instruct the blindfolded player on blowing the cup to the finish line. I made four usable blindfolds out of an old towel using elastic from some old clothes. Not only did the students enjoy playing this relay blindfolded, but they literally beg me to do many of the other relays using the blindfolds too. And since many relays can be adapted using a blindfold, it turned out that the twenty minutes it took me to make them was an excellent investment.

beanbag balance relay (k-up)

Body Awareness: balancing objects on different body parts
Equipment: one beanbag per team

Procedure: Divide your class into two or more teams. The object of this relay is to have each team member try and balance the beanbag from the starting line to a designated turning point and back. If the beanbag falls off, the student must pick it up and place it back on her head before moving on. The students are not allowed to hold the beanbag on their heads with their hands. One way to encourage students to not use their hands is to have them keep their hands behind their backs.

Variations: This relay can be creatively changed into a number of other exciting activities. The following are a few samples:

1. Use the beanbag and balance it on other body parts. Try using a shoulder balance relay. Place the beanbag on a shoulder and run the relay as above. Using the back of the hand, the elbow, or the back or the neck all give a different type of relay action.

2. Carry the beanbag under the chin. This relay is achieved by placing the beanbag under the student's chin and running to the turning point and back.

3. Frog Hop Relay: Place the beanbag between the student's knees. The students have to hop to a turning point and back without letting the beanbag drop.

sack-race relay (k-up)

Body Awareness: jumping skills
Equipment: one burlap sack per team

Procedure: Divide the class into two or more teams. Each team lines up in a single file behind a starting line. The first player is given the sack and steps into it. On a signal, the first player has to hop to the turning point and back to his team. He then gives the sack to the next player. The game continues with each player stepping into the sack and hopping around the turning point and back.

   If you happen to have a few burlap bags that have holes in the bottoms of them, you can try the next activity.

three-legged relay (k-up)

Social Awareness: sharing and cooperating
Equipment: one burlap bag per team

Procedure: Divide your class into two teams. Each team is broken down into pairs. On a signal, the first pair places their inside legs in the burlap sack. They then have to walk around a designated turning point and back to their team. They walk by holding the bag with their inside hands and stepping together first with their inside feet and then with their outside feet.

zigzag relay (k-up)

Body Awareness: using lateral movement with running
Equipment: twelve traffic cones

Procedure: In this relay the players have to run through a zigzag maze to a turning line and back again. Arrange the cones so that each team has its own zigzag course in front of it. On a signal, the first player runs the course and tags the hand of the next player. The first team to finish has to wait for the rest of the class to run the course.

snow-shoes relay (2-up)

Cognitive Awareness: math facts
Equipment: two shoeboxes per team; flash cards of math facts

Procedure: This is an excellent rainy-day activity. Divide your classroom into two groups. Using the shoebox top and bottom as snow shoes, the first players start to walk to a designated turning point and back to their group.

   Your students will soon find that the best method to travel by snow shoes is the quick shuffle step.

Variations: Another interesting idea is to have a pile of snowflake-shaped flash cards at the turning point. Each player has to pick one of the flashcards and show it to the next player in line. That player has to give the correct answer to the teacher in order for the "snow shoed" player to return and tag the next player.

Another variation is to create a rescue dog relay. In this relay, the students place their hands in the shoeboxes and walk across the room on all fours. An additional novelty is to make a paper keg that each player has to hang around his neck. In this way, the fun is to watch each player as he exchanges the barrel kegs and the snow shoes.

iceberg relay (2-up)

Body Awareness: balancing and coordinating large-muscle group
Equipment: construction paper "icebergs"; scissors

Procedure: Divide your class into two groups. The students must use the icebergs to get across the raging sea to a turning point and back to their group. The first players have a set of two icebergs. By placing the first iceberg on the ground, the player can step on it and place the second iceberg further on toward the turning point. Each player must step only on the icebergs as she tries to get from the starting line and back again. The activity continues until all the students have had a chance to participate.

chalkboard relay (2-up)

Cognitive Awareness: addition facts
Equipment: chalkboard; one piece of chalk per team

Procedure: Divide your class into two or more teams. The first player of each team runs up to the chalkboard and writes a two-digit number. When the first player returns and tags the next player, the next player runs up to the chalkboard and writes another two-digit number directly under the first player's. This continues with each player writing a different two-digit number under his team members' numbers. The last players in each group run up to the chalkboard and add all the numbers in their team's row. The first team to finish receives one point. Any team that correctly answers its problem receives two points. Remind the students to write the numbers so that team members can read them.

four-corner relay (2-up)

Body Awareness: baton-passing skills and running skills
Equipment: four bases; four batons

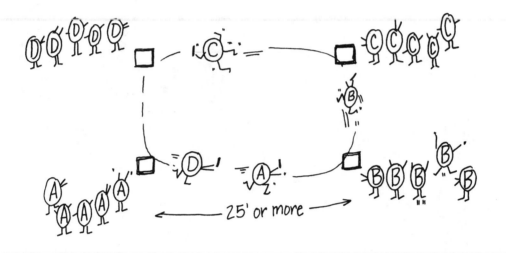

Procedure: Divide the class into four groups. Arrange the bases to form a large rectangle. Have each team line up behind one of the bases. The first player holds a passing baton for his team. On a signal, the four leaders start to run around the bases. They tag every base and pass the baton to the next player in their team. When a team finishes, all its students sit down.

cardboard-box-obstacle relay (2-up)

Body Awareness: agility and speed
Equipment: two or three large cardboard boxes per team

Procedure: Divide your class into two or more groups. Have the teams line up in a single file behind the starting line. The cardboard boxes have to be made so that the students can crawl through them. This can be done by undoing the bottom of the boxes. The boxes are placed in front of each team about ten feet apart from each other in a row. The first players must run up to and go through each of the boxes. They then run around a turning point and return to their team. Upon tagging the next player, the first runner goes to the end of the line.

ball-throw relay (2-up)

Body Awareness: ball-handling skills while running
Equipment: one ball per team

Procedure: Have the teams line up behind the starting line. The first two players on each team pass a ball back and forth between themselves as they run to the turning line and back. They must pass the ball at least eight times during this part. Upon their return, the next two players run and toss the ball to the turning line and return. This continues until all players have run. A good distance for the turning line is about twenty-five feet from the starting line.

jeremy's relay (3-up)

Body Awareness: agility and speed
Equipment: none

Procedure: This relay is named after my oldest son. Because, as a preschooler, he enjoyed running around in a circle in our kitchen at home, I decided to make up a relay that has running around in a circle as its main activity. Have students in each row of desks serve as teams. The first player in the line has to run around her group's seats and return to her own seat. The next player then runs around the seats and returns to his chair. This continues until every student has had a chance to run around his row of chairs.
 This relay can also be played if the students are standing in parallel lines.

balloon-bust relay (3-up)

Social Awareness: interacting with groups
Equipment: one balloon per student

Procedure: Divide your class into two groups. In front of each group is a chair. On a signal, the first players in the groups have to run to the chair with their balloons and sit down on them causing the balloons to break. The players then return to their group and tag the next player to run. This player and succeeding ones do the same thing with the balloons. The first group finished wins.

alphabet word race (3-up)

Cognitive Awareness: spelling words
Equipment: chalkboard; chalk

Procedure: Divide your class into three or more groups. The first players have to run to the chalkboard and write a word that begins with the letter "a." They run back and tag the next player. The next player has to go to the board and write a word that begins with the letter "b." This continues until all 26 letters of the alphabet are used to write words.

picket-fence relay (3-up)

Social Awareness: cooperating in a group
Equipment: one traffic cone per group

Procedure: Divide your class into two groups. Each team lines up as shown.
      The first player runs around the marker and places his arm to the wall. The next player runs as soon as the leader touches the wall. She goes under the arm of the first player and holds his hand. That will signal the next player to run. This continues until every player has had a turn to run.

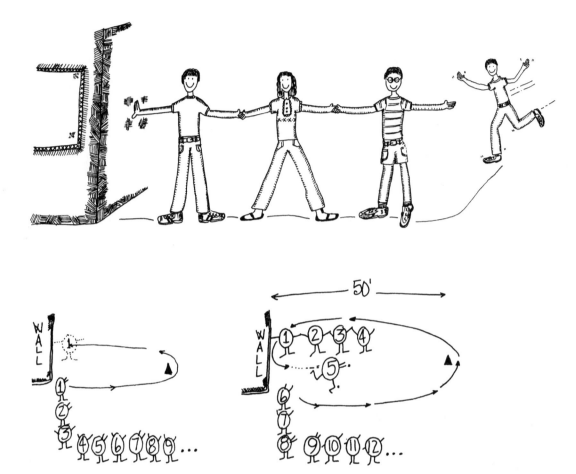

jump-rope relay (3-up)

Body Awareness: using jump rope skills
Equipment: one rope per team

Procedure: Divide your class into several small groups. The first players must run to their jump ropes about thirty feet in front of each group. They must then do five jumps and return to the group. The first group finished are the winners.

Here are other rope relay suggestions:

1. Jump five times on your left leg.
2. Jump backwards five times.
3. Jump rope and say the five times table to sixty. Say one number each time you jump.

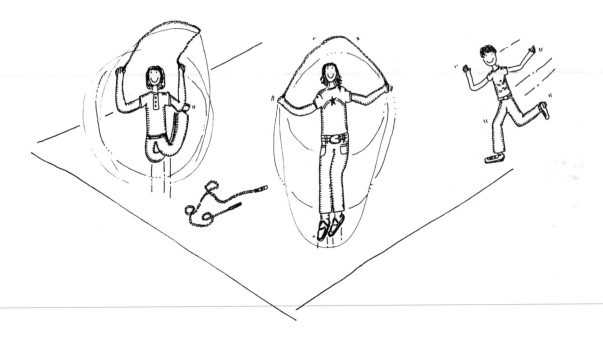

water relay (3-up)

Body Awareness: balancing
Equipment: one small paper cup per team; one bucket of water per team; one tall plastic cup per team

Procedure: This activity can be done during a hot day in spring or fall. Each group has to try and fill up a glass that is placed several yards in front of the group. The first players dip the paper cup in their bucket, place the cup on their head and walk to the glass.

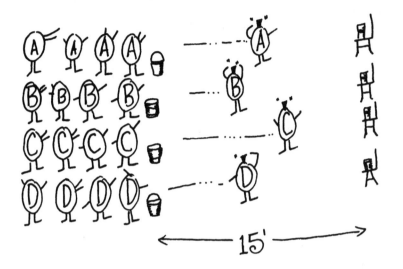

Once next to the glass, they can remove the cup and pour the water in the glass. Then they run back to give the paper cup to the next player in line. The first group to fill up their plastic glass is the winner.

carry relay (3-up)

Body Awareness: agility and speed
Equipment: books, rulers, balls, erasers, and a variety of other objects; traffic cones

Procedure: Divide your class into two groups. Place several objects in front of each group at ten-foot intervals. On a signal, the first players must run, pick up each object, and circle around the turning marker. On their return run, the players return the objects in the order that they belong. Then the players run back to their groups and tag the next player to run. This continues until a group is finished.

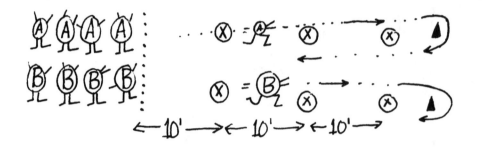

For added fun, place many objects for each player to hold.

back-and-forth relay (3-up)

Body Awareness: running skills while changing directions
Equipment: basketball court

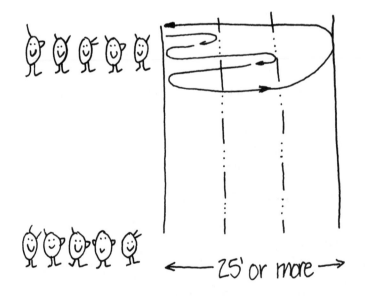

Procedure: Divide your class into two or more teams. Draw several chalk lines on the basketball court. In this relay, the first player runs to the first line, touches it, and runs back to the starting line. He then runs to the second line, touches it, and returns to the starting line again. He then runs to the last turning line, touches it, and returns to his team and tags the next player.

corner spry (3-up)

Body Awareness: throwing and catching skills
Equipment: one beanbag per team

Procedure: Divide your class into four or more teams. Each team has a Leader who stands about ten feet in front of each group. On a signal, the Leader throws the beanbag to the player at the far left of the group. The beanbag is then handed down the row until it reaches the last player. The last player runs to take the Leader's place. The old Leader then runs and stands at the far left of the group. The relay continues as the new Leader throws the beanbag to the group again. It is passed down the line to the last player. This player takes the place of the Leader as the game begins again.

      The first team to get its Leader in front again should sit down and wait for the rest of the teams to finish.

chapter SIX

In teaching any subject, it is important to provide your students with the proper skill progression. This is especially helpful in the area of physical education. Your students will find many of the traditional team sports more enjoyable if they are given the opportunity to learn basic skills in easy lead-up activities. These lead-up games will allow the students to practice their skills in progressive activities to help them master the important skills.

I remember my own fright as a youngster in third grade, in being expected to know how to bat, throw, and successfully catch a softball (that was not very soft!) in my first exposure to the game. It was a terrible experience. Many of you probably remember similar disasters. By using a wide variety of lead-up games, to softball (and other sports), you will be able to expose your students to a gradual progressive learning experience that will ensure a more successful and enjoyable time for everyone.

Chapter 6 offers a wide range of enrichment activities to provide the foundation of skills needed to play basketball, softball, football, volleyball, and soccer. Each section's activities are given in the order of progression that should be used with the students.

These games and activities should be taught to grades 3 to 6. While many of them can be adapted to the lower grades, the older students will probably find them more enjoyable.

The game of basketball had its beginnings in the state of Massachusetts. It was invented by James Naismith as an alternative game that could be played indoors during the winter months. James Naismith, a YMCA director, used peach baskets as goals, and so the game was first called "basket" ball!

Since its invention in 1891, basketball has become one of the most popular American sports.

basketball snatch and shoot (3-up)

Body Awareness: dribbling and shooting skills
Equipment: two basketballs; two hula hoops; basketball court

Procedure: This activity is played on a basketball court. Each team lines up on either side of the center court line, about fifteen feet away from each other. The two balls are placed inside the hoops on the center court line. The players on each team are numbered consecutively so that there is a matching player on each team. The teacher calls out a number, and the players with that number run up to the basketballs and dribble one ball back toward the basket on their side. They then attempt to make a basket. If a player makes a basket, he scores one point for his team. He then retrieves the ball and dribbles it back to the hoop. The player who places the ball inside the hoop first receives one point.

Total the number of points each player receives after each round. The team with the highest score wins.

dribble tag (3-up)

Body Awareness: dribbling and running skills
Equipment: four basketballs; basketball court

Procedure: This game is played on a basketball court. Select four players to be It. These four players will have the basketballs. It is up to them to dribble the ball and try to tag as many players as possible. The players who are tagged must sit down. While it may not seem fair that the taggers must dribble the basketball, the four players can easily "track down" certain players by cooperating together.

You can also play another variation of this game by having eight players being It. These eight players can then dribble *and* pass the basketball in attempts to tag the other players. Once again, the taggers must be dribbling the ball when tagging the other students.

Once all the students have been tagged, start the game over by selecting new players to be It.

boundary ball (3-up)

Body Awareness: dribbling, passing, and shooting skills
Equipment: one basketball; basketball court

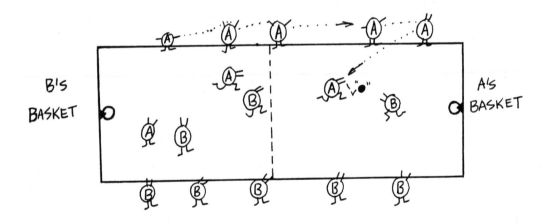

Procedure: This activity takes place on a basketball court. Divide your class into two teams. Each team lines up along the sidelines on opposite sides of the court. Three players from each team are selected to be the players on the basketball court. This game is similar to the actual game of basketball. The players on the court try and score a basket. The players on the sides of the court can help their inside players by catching and passing the ball down their line. For example, if one of the players on the basketball court is made to stop his dribble, he *must* pass the ball to one of the players on his team on the sidelines. The sideline player with the ball then passes the ball to the next player on her team. As the sideline players pass the ball down toward their basket, the players in the court will position themselves to receive a pass from the last sideline player who is nearest to their basket.

This last sideline player then throws the ball to one of her inside players on the court. The inside player can dribble or shoot the ball in the basket. When a basket is scored, three new inside players come in from the sideline for each team. The inside players go to the ends of their lines.

This is an interesting game. The players on the sidelines are involved with the game by passing the basketball toward their respective basket, and the players on the court are involved with the game by dribbling, rebounding, shooting, and trying to block throws from the outside and inside players.

You can modify this activity by allowing more than three players to be on the inside court and/or setting a certain playing time for each group to be on the court. By rotating each group every three minutes, you should be able to have every player play at least six minutes during a thirty-minute game.

The team that scores the most points during the game is the winner.

hoop ball (3-up)

Body Awareness: guarding, dribbling, and passing skills
Equipment: one basketball; two bowling pins; basketball court

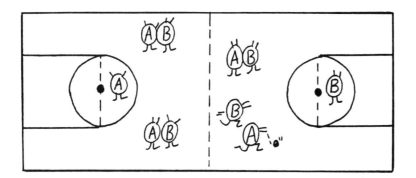

Procedure: This game is a good one to introduce your students to the actual game of basketball. There are five players on each team. The players are matched so that each player has to guard another. A pin marker is placed in the two free-throw jump circles on either side of the court. Each pin is guarded by a player from each team. Only the pin guard is allowed to be in the circle.

The object of the game is to knock down the opponent's pin or marker with the ball. The game is started by a jump ball in the center of the court. The players then try to dribble the ball or throw the ball to players who are close to the opponent's pin. The ball is then thrown to knock down the pin. If this is done, the player scores two points for her team. If the guard accidentally knocks down the pin, this scores one point for the other team.

Try to follow the other rules of basketball in this game. If a player touches the student with the ball, the student is awarded a "free throw" from the center court line. He can try and knock down the unguarded pin for one point.

The first team to score twenty-one points is the winner.

nine-court basketball (3-up)

Body Awareness: guarding, dribbling, passing, and shooting skills
Equipment: one basketball; masking tape; basketball court

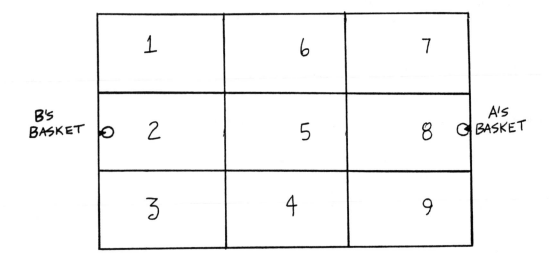

Procedure: The game is very much like the regular game of basketball. The basketball court is divided into nine different areas. One player from each team is placed in each area. This makes this activity a good game for 18 players.

The two players in the center box jump the ball into play. The ball is dribbled and passed to a player in one of the boxes that are close to the basket. Score two points for each basket made. The only limitation on this game is that the players cannot leave their assigned boxes.

When a basket is scored, all the players rotate up one number. The two players in box number 1 will go to box number 9.

Play a thirty-minute game. The team with the most points at the end of the game is the winner.

five passes (3-up)

Body Awareness: dribbling and passing skills
Equipment: one basketball; basketball court

Procedure: This is an interesting and simple activity. The object of the game is to complete five passes. When this is done the team scores one point. The game is started with a jump ball at the center jump circle. Using all the regular basketball rules, one team attempts to make five successful passes. The other team tries to steal the ball from its opponents. The team with the ball will count aloud for every pass it makes. Once a team scores a point, the other team gets to in-bound the ball. This activity is great for working on alert passing and catching skills and is an excellent way to work on good defensive quickness and ball handling awareness.

Remember, the team has to make five passes in a row. If the passes are interrupted by an opponent, the count starts over.

one bounce, no bounce (4-up)

Body Awareness: rebounding and shooting skills
Equipment: one basketball; basketball court

Procedure: Play this activity with no more than ten players at a time—the smaller the group, the better. Have your students number off in order. The first player will take a shot from the free-throw line. The player who is next will have to retrieve the ball in the following manner: If a basket is made, the next player has to catch the ball before the basketball hits the ground (no bounce). If a basket is not made, the next player must catch the ball after the first bounce (one bounce). After a successful catch, the player can take a shot from anywhere on the court. If the ball is not successfully retrieved, the player does not get a chance to shoot in that round.

The play continues until a player gets five baskets.

squad ball (4-up)

Body Awareness: guarding, dribbling, passing, and shooting skills
Equipment: one basketball; basketball court

Procedure: All the basketball rules should be followed, except for the following score changes:

If the ball hits the rim, one point is scored.

If the ball goes in the basket, the team is given two points.

This modification of the scoring rules is an attempt to encourage the players of lesser skill to try to take a shot too. Encourage every player to take the chance of scoring whenever possible.

Divide your class into four groups. Number each player and have the groups sitting along the sidelines. Begin the game by having the four number 1 players playing against the four number 2 players. Use a jump ball to start the game. The first team to score three points remains on the court to play team number 3. The other players return to their original places on the sidelines. Continue playing until all the students have had a chance to rotate into the activity.

The game of softball is an adaptation of our national sport of baseball. Softball was invented to provide a more recreational and coed sport for players of all ages and sizes. In fact, softball's original name was "playground ball," since it was the favorite of many recreational centers and schools. Today's softball is a fast-paced sport that is enjoyed by millions of school-aged youngsters throughout the world.

hot-potato-circle catch (2-up)

Body Awareness: catching and throwing skills
Equipment: two foam rubber balls or two softballs

← 30' or more →

Procedure: Have the class form a large circle with the students facing toward the center. Divide the class into two teams with members in alternate positions along the circle. Select two team Captains for this activity. At the start of the game these two players stand back-to-back in the center of the circle. The object of the game is to have the Captains throw the ball to a team member, who then tosses the ball back to the Captain. The Captain throws the ball to the next player on his team. This is continued in a clockwise fashion around the circle. Each team tries to overtake the ball of its opponent. The team that overtakes the other team's ball first wins.

New team Captains can be selected when one team overtakes the other.

Allow your students to play nine innings or rounds of this activity. You can encourage different throws (overhand, underhand, side arm) for each inning.

four-corner running (2-up)

Body Awareness: running skills
Equipment: four bases

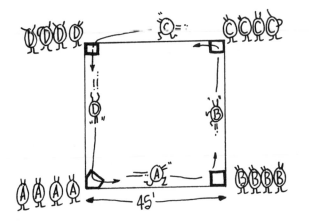

Procedure: This is an exciting relay activity. Divide your class into four groups. Each group lines up behind one of the four bases. On a signal, the first players of each group run the bases. Remind the players to tag every base. Award points to the players during each round or have a complete relay race and award points to the team.

First place = 10 points

Second place = 8 points

Third place = 6 points

Fourth place = 4 points

batting rotation (3-up)

Body Awareness: batting, pitching, throwing, and catching skills
Equipment: four bases; one softball for every four players; one bat for every four players

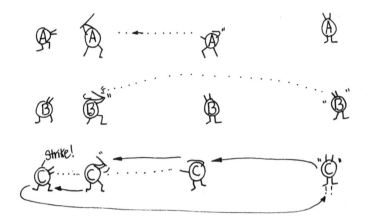

Procedure: Divide your class into groups of four players. Each group sets up in the positions as shown. There is one catcher, one batter, one pitcher, and one outfielder. The pitcher throws five good pitches to the batter. The batter hits as many as she can. Award one point to each group for every hit made by the batter. After the five pitches, the players rotate to a different position.

> The batter becomes the catcher.
>
> The catcher goes to the outfield.
>
> The outfielder becomes the pitcher.
>
> The pitcher becomes the new batter.

Besides giving points to each team for the number of hits made, you might want to give out bonus points to groups that are encouraging to each other and affirming to the players if mistakes were made.

Play until the players have had the chance to experience all the positions at least twice.

one-base softball (3-up)

Body Awareness: batting, catching, throwing, and fielding skills, and cooperating with others
Equipment: one base; one home plate; one softball; one bat

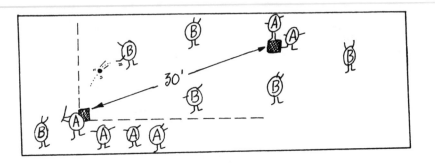

Procedure: This is an interesting and creative way to play a game using all the softball skills. One-Base Softball uses only one base instead of the normal three found in softball. The player runs to the base after a successful hit is made. The outfield team tries to get three outs on the batting team as in regulation softball. All the rules of softball apply to this game with the following exceptions:

1. Once a player makes it to the base, he does not have to run home if the next batter makes another successful hit. There can be as many players on the base as necessary.

2. The outfield team needs to tag the batter with the ball to make an out. There are no "forced outs" as in regular softball. The outfield team can still catch a fly ball for an out.

This lead-up game can provide your students with hours of enjoyment. Encourage your students to be careful and think of the times when it might be wiser to stay on the base than to run home for a score. The outfield team should be on the watch for possible double or triple plays when there are many players on the base who might run home after a successful hit.

carolina-line ball (3-up)

Body Awareness: batting and fielding skills
Equipment: one softball; one bat; three traffic cones

Procedure: This is a softball batting activity that your students will find challenging. Divide your class into two teams. The outfield team sets up the markers as shown. The object of the game is to score points by hitting the ball past the markers. The infield team scores points in the following way:

One point if the ball is hit on the ground or in the air past the first marker.

Two points if the ball is hit in the air past the second marker.

Three points if the ball is hit in the air past the third marker.

The outfield team can make outs either by catching a fly ball or fielding a ground ball before it passes the first marker. For example, if a batter hits the ball in the air past the third marker and the outfielder makes the catch, there is an out on the batting team. However, the batting team is awarded three points because the ball passed the third marker. A batter who hits the ball on the ground is awarded one point if the ball passes the first marker. If the ball continues to roll past other markers it *still counts as only one point*. On the other hand, if the ball is fielded before it passes the first marker, it is an out.

After the third out, the teams exchange places.

Encourage your students to select different outfield positions during each inning. Each outfield player should have the chance to practice catching ground and fly balls.

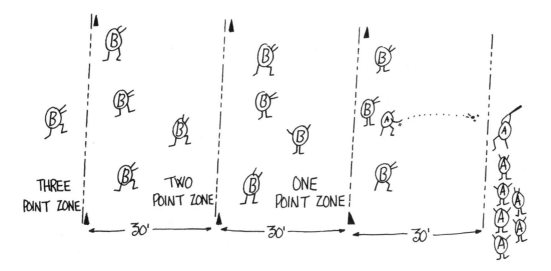

hit the bat (4-up)

Body Awareness: batting and catching skills
Equipment: one softball; one bat

Procedure: This softball activity has been a proven favorite. It is a small-group game that can be played by as few as two players. One player is selected to be the batter. The rest of the players spread out in the field. The batter hits the softball as far as she can by tossing the ball up in the air and hitting it with the bat. The batter remains up at bat until one of the outfielders catches a fly ball. If a fly ball is caught, the batter and the outfielder exchange places.

There is another way to become the batter. When a ground ball is hit, the fielder gets a chance to roll the ball at the bat that is placed at the feet of the batter. The length of the bat should be placed to face the fielder so that he has the best chance to hit the bat with the ball. The ball must be thrown from the place where the ball was fielded. The fielder cannot move closer to the bat. If the ball hits the bat, the two players exchange places. If the ball hops over the bat, or misses the bat, the batter remains.

Your older students can make this game a little harder by requiring that the batter be able to keep her position if she can successfully catch the ball as it bounces off the bat.

softball bottle bop (4-up)

Body Awareness: batting, throwing, catching, running, and pitching skills
Equipment: one softball; one bat; four bases; four 2-liter plastic soda bottles

Procedure: This game is played on a softball diamond. The game follows all the general rules of softball with the following changes due to the use of the bottles on the bases:

1. A plastic soda bottle or other similar object is placed on each of the bases and home plate. Put a few ounces of sand in each bottle to weigh them down.

2. The outfield team gets the batters out by trying to knock down the bottles. If a batter hits a fair ball, he can be put out by knocking the bottle off the first base before he reaches it. The bottle must be knocked off with the ball that was just hit.

3. The batter does not run to each of the bases, but runs around the bases. It will be up to the teacher or appointed umpire to determine if the runner ran past the base before the bottle was knocked down. For example, if the batter hits a fair ball then he can run toward first base. The outfield team retrieves the ball and quickly relays it to a player who is in position to knock down the bottle with the ball. If the batter runs past the base before the bottle is knocked down, the batter is safe. The batter then stays at first base.

4. A batter is allowed to move ahead only one base at a time. No matter how hard the ball was hit, the batter can advance only to the next base. For example, if there was a player on first base and the batter hit the ball over the heads of the outfielders, the player on first base can advance only to second base and the batter can advance only to first base. Therefore, the outfield team must look for ways to knock down the bottle of a base that a runner must advance to. If there are players on first and second bases, the outfield team must try to knock down the bottle at third base to cause a "forced" out.

The rest of the softball rules apply to this game of Softball Bottle Bop. If a fly ball is caught, it is an out. If the batter makes three strikes, he is out. If the pitcher knocks down the bottle at home plate with a good pitch, the batter is out.

Volleyball, like basketball, is an American invention. In fact, volleyball was invented *because* of basketball. The businessmen who used the YMCAs and other sports clubs started to complain that basketball was too vigorous an activity for them to play during their usual lunch-hour recreational activity. They wanted an activity that would have many players on each team, but would not have all the running that basketball requires. So, the game of volleyball was invented by taking the inflated bladder from the inside of a leather basketball and using the lightweight bladder as the ball. The ball was hit back and forth over a net that was suspended in the air. Not only was volleyball invented because of basketball, but it was invented from a basketball.

balloon volley (2-up)

Body Awareness: striking an object over a net
Equipment: one balloon (have additional ones available in case of breakage); volleyball net

Procedure: This is a good activity to introduce your students to the concept of striking an object (a balloon) over a net. Use a net or string stretched across the playing area at a height of about six feet. Select four players to be on each team. A restraining line is drawn about eight feet back from either side of the net. This is used as the serving line. The server tries to hit the balloon over the net. Once the balloon is over the net, the other team has to volley the balloon back over to the other side. Use all the regular volleyball rules but allow the serving team an additional relay tap to get the balloon over the net on the serve. To encourage the participation of all students, you can allow up to five hits before the balloon needs to go over the net. The balloon cannot be hit by the same player twice in a row.

Use the same scoring system as in volleyball: The team with the serve can score a point by hitting the balloon over the net in such a way that it cannot be retrieved by the other team. The team that did not serve the ball does *not* get a point if their opponents are not able to hit the balloon over. Instead, that team will get the balloon to serve. Remember to rotate the players so that everyone gets a chance to serve the balloon.

newcomb (3-up)

Body Awareness: using all volleyball skills in a game situation; tracking the ball
Equipment: one volleyball; volleyball net

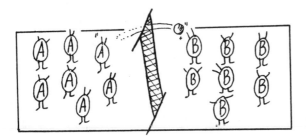

Procedure: Newcomb is played on a regular volleyball court area. It is played with all the volleyball rules except that the players are allowed to catch the volleyball. Select two teams of between eight to twelve players on a team. The players are scattered on their side of the volleyball court at equal distances from their teammates. The players should keep to their assigned area and not interfere with other players.

The object of the game is to throw the ball over the net into the opponent's court. The opponents must catch the ball before it hits the ground.

Once the volleyball has been thrown over the net, the other team can take up to three passes to throw the ball back over. For example, if the ball was caught near the back of the volleyball court, the person who caught the ball might want to throw the ball to another player closer to the net.

All the passes should be done quickly. The play should be rapid and continue until a point is scored or the serve is lost to the other team.

A player with the ball is not allowed to move.

Start the game by having the volleyball thrown over the net by a player standing behind the serving line. The ball may be relayed to a closer player if the server feels she cannot throw the ball over on one attempt.

one-bounce ball (4-up)

Body Awareness: hitting a ball over the net
Equipment: one volleyball; volleyball net

Procedure: This game is played on a volleyball court area. The difference in this game is that the net is lowered so that it is about four feet high and the ball is allowed one bounce before it needs to be hit. Assign six players on each team. The object of the game is to hit the ball over the net into the opponent's court. A team is given up to three hits to do this. Each hit can be taken off a bounce. For example, the team that was served the ball can allow the ball to bounce one time on their side before the ball is hit over the net or to another teammate. Every subsequent hit can be taken after the ball has bounced one time. All the regular rules of volleyball apply to this activity. The "one-bounce" rule and the lowered net make this game more interesting and suitable for the elementary-age youngster.

four-court volleyball (4-up)

Body Awareness: hitting a ball over the net
Equipment: one volleyball; four volleyball nets

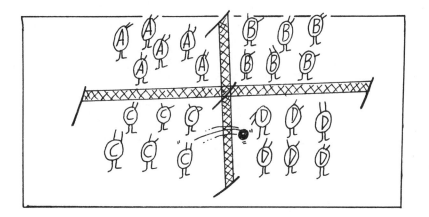

Procedure: This activity is great because it can accommodate a large number of students as players. The four nets are placed so that there are four individual sections for four teams to play in. Each team can consist of between six to nine players. All the volleyball rules apply in this activity.

The object of the game is to hit the ball over the net into one of the three other courts. Any player can return the ball on a volley to one of the other three courts. Because there are four courts, the game is a very interesting one. All the players in all courts have to be alert, for while the ball might be hit back and forth between two teams for a while, a student never knows when the ball might be hit into his court.

The scoring system is simple. If a player on a team causes the ball to go out of bounds or a team does not return the ball over the net, the team is given one point. The team with the lowest score at the end of the playing time is the winner.

surprise ball (4-up)

Body Awareness: quickness and agility
Equipment: one volleyball; volleyball net; a blanket or sheet

Procedure: This exciting game will develop quickness in your students. The volleyball net is draped with the sheet so that each team cannot see the other players.

The object of the game is to throw the volleyball back and forth over the sheet that hides the two teams from each other. The person who catches the ball quickly throws the ball back over the net. If you want to play with large numbers of students, just enlarge the playing area to have a deeper restraining line. You might also want to add another ball to make the action faster paced. Encourage the students to throw the ball to different parts of the court to confuse their opponents. As the students get better at quickly throwing the ball to different areas, the other players have to become more alert to make a successful catch.

Award one point to the opponents whenever the ball falls to the ground or is thrown out of bounds. Play until one side scores fifteen points.

ADDITIONAL SUGGESTIONS

Here are a few additional suggestions for adapting volleyball rules to suit your students. Volleyball is a game that needs various modifications so that your students will feel successful at it.

1. Allow several trial serves for each student before the real serve.
2. Allow the server to hit the ball from the middle of his court instead of from the serving line.
3. Give your students an unlimited number of hits before the ball needs to be hit over the net.
4. Allow the same player to hit the volleyball up to three times in a row.
5. Lower the net to match the level of their abilities.

The game of football is played almost exclusively in the countries of Canada and the United States. In other parts of the world—South America and Europe—the word "football" is used to describe what we know as soccer. It is generally agreed that soccer was the game from which football evolved. As the story goes, in 1823, two college teams were playing a game of soccer. A player from the team of Rugby College was so upset with his team's performance that he picked up the ball and ran with it. Soon all the soccer players in England were telling of the way that soccer was "played at Rugby."

Of course, Rugby soon became a very popular sport in England, with the round soccer ball being replaced by an oval ball that could be easily held while running. In time, football developed from the sport of Rugby.

Harvard University was the site of the first official football game, in the year 1874. Today football is one of the most popular sports in America.

ten points (3-up)

Body Awareness: catching, throwing, and hiking skills
Equipment: one football per group

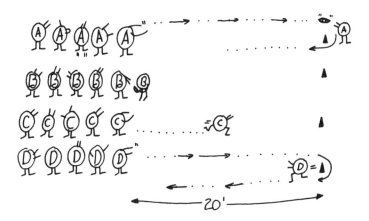

Procedure: This is an interesting football relay activity. Divide your students into two or more groups. Each group is given a football. The groups form into single files. On a signal, the first player hikes the ball to the player behind him. The first player then runs to a designated catching line. The second player passes the football to the first player. If the ball is caught, the player scores one point for his team. The first player runs back to his group and gives the ball to the next player in line. The relay continues with the ball being hiked to the new passer, who will throw the ball to the player at the catching line. The first team to score ten points should quietly wait until all the groups are finished.

touchdown! (3-up)

Body Awareness: tagging a runner; catching and running with the ball
Equipment: one football

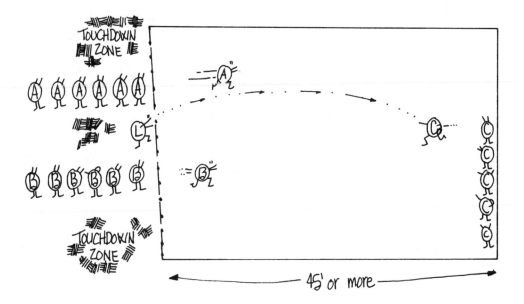

Procedure: Divide your class into three groups. These groups line up in the formation shown. The teacher or leader throws the ball to the first player in group C. This player then tries to run to the touchdown area without being tagged by the two players from groups A and B. The two taggers start their pursuit after the football is received by the player.

     The group that is running with the ball is given points if the runner is able to elude the two taggers and reach the touchdown zone.

     Score six points if the runner gets to the touchdown zone safely without being tagged by either player.

     Score three points if the runner gets to the touchdown area and is tagged by only one player. If both taggers are successful, the runner scores no points.

     This continues until all the players in group C are given a chance to run with the ball. Rotate the players so that every group gets to run the ball back for points.

who has the football? (3-up)

Body Awareness: tagging and running skills
Equipment: one tennis ball; goal markers

Procedure: This activity is good for introducing your students to proper tagging techniques. Players should be able to tag one another without pushing or hitting. This game is played with two teams of between five to twelve players. The teams line up opposite each other. The two groups should be about 100 feet apart. Behind each team are the designated goals. They can be marked with traffic cones or other objects.

One team is given the tennis ball. This team huddles up and gives the ball to one of its players. The team breaks the huddle and all the players run toward the goal line. Each student pretends that he has the tennis ball. The players on the opposite team try and tag the player who really has the ball. If the player with the ball gets to the goal line without being tagged, he scores six points for his team.

This action is repeated with the other team given the chance to huddle up and score a touchdown. The team with the most points at the end of the game is the winner.

line up (3-up)

Cognitive Awareness: knowing football positions and their names
Equipment: one football

Procedure: This activity can be used to acquaint your students with the various positions in football and their names. Many of your students will be aware of the various positions that football players can take. Following are the names of a typical formation:

1. The Center takes his position directly in front of the ball. He is the player who hikes the ball to the Quarterback when his team has the ball.

2. On each side of the Center are the two Guards. The Right Guard is on the right-hand side of the center and the Left Guard is on the other side.

3. The two Tackles are on the left and right side of the Guards.

4. The two Ends are on the outside of the Tackles. The Ends are the players to whom the football is usually passed.

5. The Quarterback stands behind the center. He is the player who passes the ball.

6. On each side of the Quarterback are the two Halfbacks.

7. The Halfbacks, along with the Fullback, are the players who usually run with the ball. The Fullback lines up behind the Quarterback.

While there are many football formations, you can use this one to explain to your students the traditional offensive formation.

Line Up is an activity that will allow your students to practice their formations. Assign each player a position on one of two football teams. These two teams are lined up facing each other with a fifty-foot distance separating them.

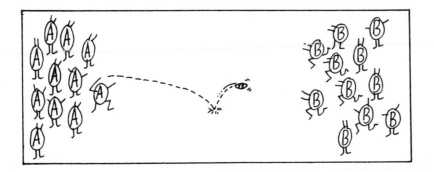

One team is given the football. One player on that team throws the football toward the other team. The other team retrieves the ball and places the ball on the ground. Both teams quickly form their positions on their side of the football. The first team to correctly form the lineup is given one point. The two teams then take their original positions as the other team gets to throw the football.

Play until one team scores five points.

run back (3-up)

Body Awareness: running skills and grabbing a flag
Equipment: football flags

Procedure: This activity will introduce your students to the use of football flags. Flags are used in the game of flag football. Each student will have a flag belt on. The flags on the belt are easily detachable and are grabbed off by an opponent in lieu of tagging. Divide the class into two groups. All students should have their own flags if enough are available.

Both groups line up on opposite ends of the football field. On a signal, both teams run toward each other. The object of the activity is to see how many opponent's flags they can capture while running toward their end zone. The students try to keep their opponents from grabbing their flags, while trying to get flags from other opponents.

Count the number of players on each team who are able to reach the end zone with their flags.

easy football (4-up)

Body Awareness: punting and throwing skills
Equipment: one football; football field

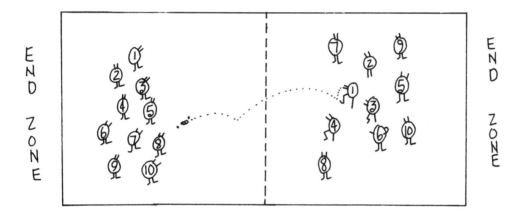

Procedure: This activity is played on a football field. Assign eight players to a team. Each team is arranged on its own side of the football field. Each player on the team should be numbered in order. The first player of one team is given the ball. She punts the ball as far as she can. The members on the opposite team quickly field the football so that it does not go far into their territory. The first player on their team then punts the football as far as he can. The game continues with each team punting the football from the spot where the ball was recovered. The object of the game is to be the first team to kick the football into the end zone. As the players from each team kick the ball in their numbered order, each player tries to out-kick his counterpart on the opposite team.

When a team is close to its goal line, the player can attempt to kick the ball into the end zone. If the ball gets into the end zone, that team wins the game.

This game can also be played by having the players throw the ball instead of punting the ball into the end zone.

fun football (4-up)

Body Awareness: passing, running, catching, intercepting, and tagging skills
Equipment: one football; football field

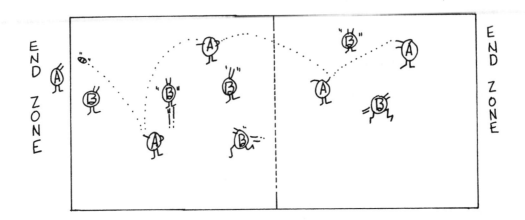

Procedure: This game resembles a huge "keep-away" game. Select two teams having eight to ten players. The football is given to one team. Each team lines up on opposite ends of the football field. The team with the ball tries to pass it from player to player. The other team tries to intercept the ball. The team with the ball tries to get the ball to the opposite end zone.

The football is moved down the field in the following manner:

1. The players with the ball pass the ball from player to player. The player with the ball is able to run with it until she is tagged by an opponent. Once she is tagged, she has to quickly throw the ball to one of her teammates.

2. If the ball is caught by a teammate, that player is allowed to run until he is tagged. If the ball was just picked up from the ground where it fell after a player did not catch it, the player cannot run. He will have to pass the ball to another player.

3. If the ball is intercepted, that player is allowed to run until he is tagged by an opponent. If a player steals the ball off the ground, then he must stop and throw the ball to another player.

4. This will continue until the football is either passed into the end zone or a player is able to run into the end zone.

After a touchdown is scored, the other team is given the ball to start another round of play. Encourage your students to play this game using good sportsmanship and regard for the rules. Students may need to be reminded to keep from "ganging up" on the person with the ball. Once the player has been tagged, she should be given enough room to make a throw.

When a touchdown is made, the other team is given the ball and the chance to pass and run.

everyone's eligible (4-up)

Body Awareness: catching, throwing, and running skills
Equipment: one football; football field

Procedure: This activity is played according to all the regular touch football rules except that all the players are eligible to receive the football. In regular football, only the backs and the ends are able to catch the ball and run with it. By having all the players eligible, you create a more inviting situation for all your students.

Select two teams of up to eleven players on each team.

FURTHER IDEAS ON MODIFYING FOOTBALL

Here are a few more ideas on how to modify the rules or equipment to better meet the needs of your students:

1. Use a foam-rubber football instead of a harder one. You will find that more students enjoy using a softer ball.

2. Use a "soft rush" rule. In football, a lot of students will not like the contact after the time when the ball is hiked to the Quarterback. Instead of having the players on defense rushing in to try to get the Quarterback, have a rule that says the defensive team has to count to three before they can rush in. This allows the Quarterback the chance to try to complete the pass more easily. It also places more stress on intercepting the ball instead of having your students all rushing in after the Quarterback.

3. Encourage your students to rotate all the positions among themselves. Each player should be given the chance to play all the different positions.

Soccer has become one of the most popular sports in the United States during the past ten years. Because soccer uses the basic movement skills of running and kicking, it has great appeal for players of all ages.

The innovative concept of multiaged and coed soccer participation has helped soccer to develop as a family recreational activity.

You can help your students enjoy this activity!

obstacle dribble (2-up)

Body Awareness: dribbling skills
Equipment: one soccer ball per group; several traffic cones

Procedure: Divide your class into two or more squads. Each group lines up in a file in the pattern shown. The first player dribbles the ball in and out of the cones and then back to the next player. Students should have control of the ball at all times. This makes an excellent relay activity.

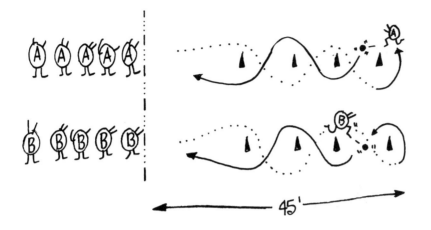

goal attack (2-up)

Body Awareness: dribbling and goal-shooting skills
Equipment: one soccer ball per group; two traffic markers

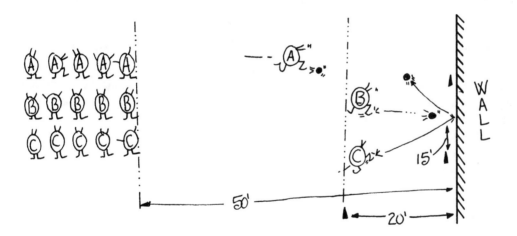

Procedure: Select players to be in two or more groups. Each group lines up in a single file. The first players dribble the ball until they reach a designated goal-kicking area. They then try to kick the ball between the markers for a goal. The players should then retrieve their ball and dribble it to the next player.

Use this activity first as a skill-building exercise and then as a fun relay.

black bottom (3-up)

Body Awareness: kicking skills
Equipment: one semideflated soccer ball

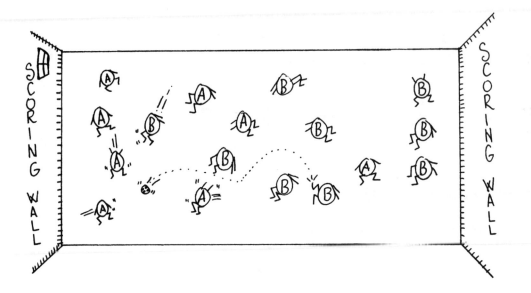

Procedure: This is an indoor activity that is loads of fun. Select two teams. The teams scatter themselves inside the gym area. The object of the game is to kick the ball across the gym to score a point by having the ball hit the wall. Unlike a regular indoor soccer game, all the players have to scoot along the gym floor in the crab position. The players are not allowed to stand up or crawl on their knees.

The game is started by throwing the ball in the center of the gym. The players then try to kick the ball toward their scoring wall. Score one point for a goal. Play until one team scores five points.

line soccer (3-up)

Body Awareness: dribbling and kicking skills
Equipment: one soccer ball

Procedure: The class is divided into two groups and lines up as shown. Each player on both teams is numbered. A soccer ball is placed in the center of the court. The game starts with the teacher calling out two or more numbers. The players with that number try to kick the soccer ball across the opponent's restraining line for a score.

The players in the center try to steal the ball from their opponents while the rest of the players who are on the line act as goalies. The goalies try to keep the ball from passing the restraining line. They cannot use their hands but can kick the ball back into the playing area.

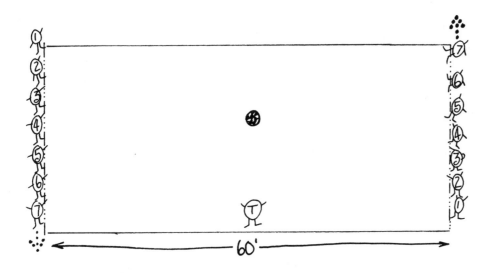

The play continues until a goal is scored. The players who were called will go back to their line, and the teacher calls out two more numbers.

Play until all the players have had at least two chances to be in the center. The team with the most points is the winner.

box soccer (3-up)

Body Awareness: dribbling and kicking skills
Equipment: one soccer ball; basketball court

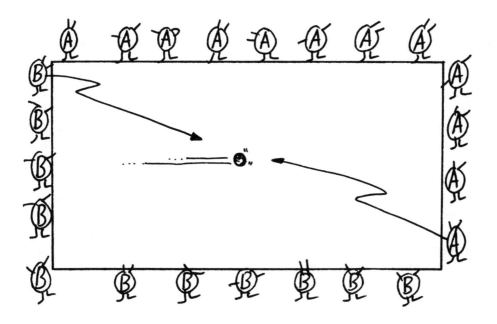

Procedure: Divide your class into two groups. The two groups line up around a basketball court playing area as shown. This is an individual scoring activity. Each player tries to score points by kicking the ball out of the playing area. The two players at the far ends of the court are the first two players. The teacher rolls the soccer ball on the court. The two players then try to be the first ones to kick the ball outside the playing area. All the other players who are standing outside the area try to block the ball from going out. After the ball has been kicked out by one of the players, all the players rotate forward to the diagonal corner. The old players go to the end of their line.

Play until all the players have had at least three chances. The players with the most points are the winners.

bowling pin soccer (3-up)

Body Awareness: dribbling and kicking skills
Equipment: one soccer ball; six bowling pins

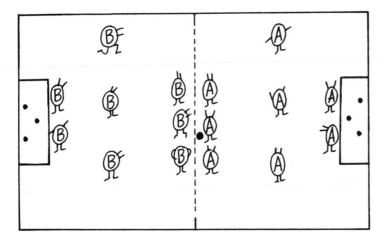

Procedure: This activity can be played indoors in a gym or out on the playground. Select eight players to be on each team. The players try to knock down the three bowling pins that are in the goal areas as shown. At either end of the playing area are the three bowling pins. You can use plastic milk jugs or other unbreakable bottles instead of the bowling pins.

This activity follows the rules of soccer. The only difference in this activity is that the teams are awarded one point for every pin that is knocked down. If the ball happens to knock down more than one pin, that team is given bonus points for each extra pin knocked down.

The game is started by giving the ball to one of the teams. The center player on the team passes the ball to one of her teammates. Each team is allowed to have up to two guards to serve as Goalies. They will try to keep the ball from entering the goal box. Only the Goalies are allowed to use their hands.

Once a point is scored, the ball is given to the other team to put into play.

Encourage your students to pass the ball to players who are in better positions to make a possible goal kick.

chapter SEVEN

STUNTS
PYRAMIDS
and other
CHALLENGES

This chapter describes many of the special stunts, contests, and other feats that challenge your students and provide them with hours of fun.

The activities, which can be done both indoors and outdoors, are divided into the following sections:

- Active Stunts for Two
- Classroom Olympics
- Tumbling, Gymnastics, and Balance Skills
- Group and Individual Challenges

bug tug (k-up)

Body Awareness: physical fitness
Equipment: none

Procedure: The two players start by standing back to back on either side of a line drawn between them. They bend forward and reach their hands down between their legs. Each player grabs the hands of the other player and tries to tug her opponent over the center line.

    This activity can be used as a warm-up exercise too.

partner ball handling (k-up)

Body Awareness: making slow, identical movements with a partner
Equipment: one utility ball

Procedure: The two players lie flat on their stomachs opposite each other. The ball is placed between their heads. The object of this activity is for the two players to try to lift the ball off the ground. The players carefully keep the ball wedged between their heads as they move from the lying position, to a crouching position, and then to a standing position.

    Try this activity using more than two players. See how many players you can get to cooperate and lift the ball.

towel tug (2-up)

Body Awareness: developing upper body fitness
Equipment: one towel

Procedure: This is a simple tug-of-war activity between two players. The two players hold on to opposite ends of an old towel. They stand on opposite sides of a line drawn between them. On a signal, the two players try to pull the other over the line. The player who pulls the other over the line is the winner.

You can have an exciting class towel tug by dividing your class into four groups. You will need one towel per group in this activity. Each group lines up in a single file. The first two players on each line will do the towel tug first. The winner of the contest gets to challenge the next player in line. The object of the activity is to stay up as the winner as long as possible. The losers of each round go to the end of line.

wring the dishrag (2-up)

Body Awareness: coordinating movements with a partner
Equipment: none

Procedure: The two players stand facing each other and hold hands. They turn their shoulders under, and raising the other joined hands, they twist in a circular motion while still holding onto their hands.

rooster fight (3-up)

Body Awareness: physical fitness
Equipment: none

Procedure: Two players enter a ten-foot diameter circle. Each player has to squat and hold on to her ankles. The object of this activity is to be the first player to bump the other out of the circle. The players have to remember to hold onto their ankles *throughout* the match. Each player is allowed three warnings before being disqualified.

Another way to do this activity is to have more than two players in the circle. As each player is driven out of the circle, that leaves the others to try to be the last one left in the circle. Five players makes a good match in a ten-foot diameter circle.

poison pin (3-up)

Body Awareness: developing basic wrestling movements
Equipment: one bowling pin

Procedure: This activity has been a long-time favorite of my students. Two players stand on opposite sides of the pin or other marker. Each student holds the hands of the other player. The object of the game is to try to force the opponent to knock down the pin with his feet. The two players push and pull each other in attempts to cause the pin to fall down.

The player who causes the other to knock down the pin is the winner.

You can have three students in a poison pin match too. This adds to the excitement by matching the two remaining players together during the next contest. If you have more than one pin, you can have several matches going on at the same time. The losers from each match can play each other in a consolation game.

hop shove (3-up)

Body Awareness: balancing skills
Equipment: none

Procedure: Two students are engaged in a mild combative event. Each player holds on to one of her ankles with one hand. The players hop on the free leg and try to bump shoulders with their opponent. The object of the game is to try to cause the other player to lose her balance and let go of her ankle. Play for the best two out of three matches.

rope wrestling (3-up)

Body Awareness: balancing skills and physical fitness
Equipment: one jump rope; two carpet squares

Procedure: Two players stand about six feet from each other, each one on a small carpet square. The rope is held in one hand of each of the players. The object of the game is to get the other player to step off the carpet square. This is a game of finesse, since one player will not be able to forcefully pull the other off the carpet square without endangering his own balance. This game calls for a more intelligent type of play than just pure strength.

towel fling (3-up)

Body Awareness: catching and throwing skills
Equipment: one towel; one utility ball

Procedure: This is another cooperative activity. Two players hold on to the ends of an outstretched towel. A ball is placed on the towel. The players must fling the ball up in the air and catch it on the towel. Challenge the players to see how many times they can catch the ball.

lame dog walk (k-1)

Body Awareness: physical fitness
Equipment: none

Procedure: This stunt is performed by having your students walking on their hands and feet. Have each student select either an arm or foot to limp with. This body part cannot be used to place weight on. You can challenge your students to see how difficult it is to walk without the use of a certain body part in this relay event. The Leader will call out the injured body part at the beginning of each relay. The students may not use that part as they compete in a relay situation.

log rolling (k-2)

Social Awareness: interacting and cooperating with a group
Equipment: none

Procedure: This is an interesting group activity. Have all your students lie down in a line on their stomachs. The players have to be very close so that the students resemble a human carpet. The first player in line starts to roll over the other players as the players turn their bodies to help her roll easily. When the first player gets to the end of the line, she lies down too. The next player then starts to roll across the rest of the group. This continues until all the players have had a chance to roll across the giant human carpet.

ping-pong-ball blow (k-3)

Social Awareness: cooperating in a group
Equipment: one Ping-Pong ball

Procedure: Select four students to play against another four-student group. Each group stands opposite the other on different sides of a large table. The object of the game is to blow the Ping-Pong ball off on the opponent's side. The ball is placed in the center of the table. On a signal, the players start to blow the ball. By having three players along the length of the table and the fourth player on either side end, the ball will soon blow off with one of the teams scoring one point. The players cannot use their hands to block the ball from falling off.

Allow each group several chances to play.

crab tag (k-3)

Body Awareness: agility and physical fitness
Equipment: none

Procedure: All your students are spread out in the playing area. They have to assume the crab-walk position—they are in a sitting position on the floor and move by using their arms and feet. On a signal, all the students see how many of the other students they can tag. Challenge them to tag at least ten players in thirty seconds.

You can play several rounds as a warm-up activity.

skier's sit (k-up)

Body Awareness: building upper-leg-muscle strength
Equipment: none

Procedure: This activity can provide an interesting break in your busy school day. While it looks easy and comfortable, the skier's sit is actually a hard exercise that will give your students great muscle tone in their legs. Have your students stand about sixteen inches from a wall. The students then sit down so that their backs are supported against the wall. As they assume a seated position, the weight of their bodies has to be supported by their legs. It may seem easy, but it is quite hard to assume this position for long periods.

heel click (k-up)

Body Awareness: coordinating gross motor movements
Equipment: none

Procedure: The heel click is performed by having the students jump up and click their heels together. If your students have an easy time at clicking their heels once, challenge them to see how many times they can click their heels together.

You can also try a heel click progression. Your students click their heels once on the first jump, then twice on the second jump. This continues until your students are unable to add a new heel click on each successive jump.

thread the needle (k-up)

Body Awareness: balancing and flexibility skills
Equipment: none

Procedure: This stunt is performed by having the students grasping their own hands together. The object of the stunt is to see if they can step through their own hands with both legs and step back out again without breaking their grasp.

thumb wrestling (2-up)

Body Awareness: coordinating fine motor movements
Equipment: none

Procedure: Have your students seated opposite their partners. They grip their right hands together by curling their fingers as they clasp fists. Both players have their thumbs pointed up. On a signal, each player tries to press his opponent's thumb down with his thumb. Your students can play several matches.

You will find that even the smaller players can be evenly matched against a bigger student. The ability of quick reactions and good eye-hand coordination is foremost in a game like this. Encourage your students to try to fake their movements so that the game becomes a tactical activity. As your students become better at the game, you'll find that a match takes several minutes. Have your students play the best out of seven games and then change partners.

seal slap (2-up)

Body Awareness: physical fitness
Equipment: none

Procedure: This physical stunt is performed by having your students assume a bent-legged push-up position. The students then try to push off the ground and slap their hands together before they touch back down to the ground. Be sure to do this activity on a soft surface.

stick pull (3-up)

Body Awareness: developing upper body strength
Equipment: several 2-foot long dowels; mats

Procedure: Have your students select partners of equal height and strength. The object of the activity is to see who can pull the other player over the designated line. The two players face each other and grasp the wooden dowel with both hands. There is a marked line three feet behind each player. On a signal, each player tries to pull the other across the designated line. Allow each pair to play three matches. Have your students change partners several times.

flower blossom (3-up)

Social Awareness: cooperating in a group
Equipment: none

Procedure: This is a great group cooperation game that is very hard to do right. Select groups of five or six students. The object of the activity is to see if all the players in the group can perform a group stand up from a sitting position. All the players form a small circle by sitting on the ground and holding each others' hands. On a signal, all the students attempt to stand up. The students should bend their legs and slowly lift up with their arms. Once a group is standing up, they have to perform the second part of the activity.

Each group tries to form the flower blossom by leaning backward and holding fast to the others' hands. This makes a beautiful group balancing act.

egg roll (k-1)

Body Awareness: tumbling skills
Equipment: mats

Procedure: An egg roll is a basic movement that is used to introduce students to a tuck roll. The students perform the skill by lying on their backs and grabbing their knees in a tight tuck position. They rock themselves from side to side to imitate the movement an egg would make. As they wobble back and forth, let the students explore rocking their bodies in various directions.

turk stand (k-2)

Body Awareness: balancing skills
Equipment: none

Procedure: Have your students sit on the floor in a cross-legged position. Each of the students should have her arms folded. The object of this balancing skill is to see how many students can rise to a standing position without unfolding her arms or legs. Once the student is up, she then sits down and returns to the original position.

front roll (k-up)

Body Awareness: tumbling skills
Equipment: mats

Contact with shoulders
and back, not head!

Procedure: The forward roll is one of the basic movements in tumbling. It can be broken down into five parts:

1. Bend forward, placing the hands on the mat . . .
2. Jump with the legs, tucking the head . . .
3. Roll on the broad part of the shoulders and back . . .
4. Tuck the body to form a ball-like shape . . .
5. Roll up to the feet to stand.

  The most important part in teaching the front roll is to encourage the student to keep his head tucked in. The chin should be touching the chest as the player rolls forward. You can use a beanbag or other object to place under the chin of those students who are having problems keeping their heads down. The beanbag is placed under the student's chin so that the student has to keep his head tucked to keep the beanbag in place.

  Another common fault is to have the student roll with his legs straight. The legs should be tucked close to the body as the student rolls to his feet. The students may want to hold onto their knees as they roll up. By grabbing their knees, the students find that their feet naturally contact the mat and that they can rise to a standing position.

back roll (k-up)

Body Awareness: tumbling skills
Equipment: mats

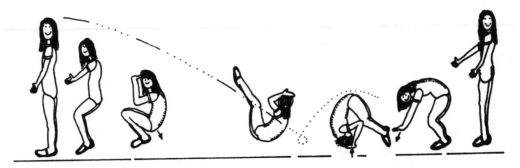

Procedure: Here's how to perform a back roll.

1. From a standing start, sit down and tuck the body into a tight ball . . .
2. Roll backwards with the hands placed on either side of the head . . .
3. When the hands come in contact with the mats, push downwards.
4. The hands will continue to be pushed downward as the feet are swung around to contact the floor.

Watch out for your students trying to "throw" their backs backwards. This will cause them to land with a hard "thump" on the mat. The back needs to remain in a tight tuck as the student rolls backwards to his hands.

airplane scale (k-up)

Body Awareness: balancing skills
Equipment: none

Procedure: This balance skill is performed on one foot. The student raises one leg behind him and leans forward. His arms should be spread out to the sides. This position will resemble an airplane. Hold this balance for ten seconds. You will be surprised how difficult it is to hold this position without moving and losing balance.

headstand (2-up)

Body Awareness: balancing skills
Equipment: mats

Procedure: The headstand is one of the easiest skills to teach, if you understand the mechanics of the balance being attempted. The mechanics of the skill are simple—keep the center of gravity of the student over the base of support.

As the student places his hands on the mat, he forms a large triangle. This triangle is the base of support. The student lifts his hips (center of gravity) over this base of support and keeps himself up by pressing down with his hands.

In the headstand, the body should be straight. There should be little or no arch in the back. Have each student select a partner to help hold his legs as the balance is attempted.

partner shoulder stand (2-up)

Body Awareness: balancing skills
Equipment: mats

Procedure: This partner balance is performed by having the bottom student supporting the shoulders of the top performer. The top performer places his hands on the knees of the bottom performer for extra support.

This stunt is started by having the top performer leaning forward and placing his hands on the knees of the bottom player. The bottom player supports the top player's shoulders.

Have extra spotters standing on either side of the top performer. These two spotters will help in case the balancing player starts to fall.

cartwheel (2-up)

Body Awareness: tumbling skills
Equipment: mats

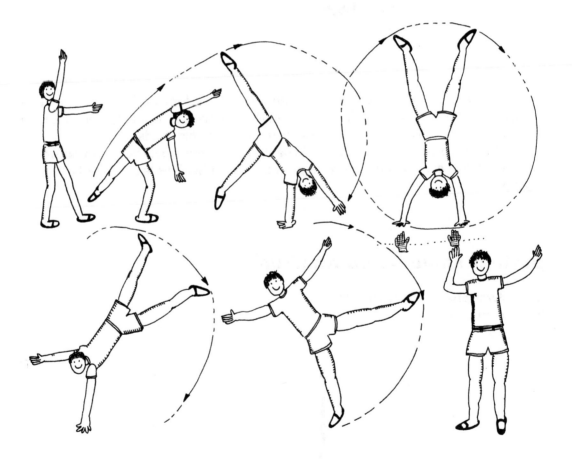

Procedure: The motion of the cartwheel is like a wheel. The body can be likened to an old-fashioned cartwheel, with the arms and legs of the student being the spokes of the wheel. The student starts this skill by placing one foot in front of the other. The arms are swung down and forward, with the hands placed on the floor one after the other. The correct hand placement should follow that of the feet. For example, if the student starts off with the left foot placed in front, then the left hand should be placed on the floor next. A common error is to place the opposite hand down on the floor first. If the left foot is led, then it is wrong to place the right hand to the ground next.

The skill is finished up by kicking both legs into the air and landing one foot at a time.

frog stand (2-up)

Body Awareness: balancing skills
Equipment: mats

Procedure: The students perform this skill by placing their hands on the ground from a squat position. The knees are placed on the elbows as the body is tipped forward to a balancing position. Your students should be able to hold this position from three to thirty seconds.

rocking chair (2-up)

Body Awareness: balancing skills
Equipment: mats

Procedure: Have your students select a partner of equal height. The two players squat and sit on each other's feet while facing each other with their knees bent. Each student holds her partner's arm above the wrist. The students try to rock back and forth. Challenge the students to rock as high as possible and still keep control over the movement.

pyramids (3-up)

Body Awareness: balancing skills
Equipment: mats

Procedure: Use the following suggestions to build a human pyramid. Remember that your students need to be familiar with all the balance skills before a pyramid is attempted. A complete mastery of the balance skills that make up the pyramids will ensure a safe and enjoyable time for your students.

THREE-PERSON PYRAMIDS

Here are a few suggestions for making three-person pyramids:

1. *The Rider Pyramid:* This is performed by having two players kneeling side by side. The third player carefully stands over the hips of the bottom performers. This resembles a person standing on two horses.

2. *The Lean-to Pyramid:* This pyramid is performed with two players doing handstands. The third player is in the middle of the two players. He holds the other players' feet with his hands.

3. *The Flying "W" Pyramid:* This is performed by having one student standing on the inside knees of the two bottom players. The player in the center places her hands together and points them straight up. The players on the bottom each hold on to the legs of the third player and extend their outside arms. This formation will resemble a "W."

4. *The Tripod Pyramid:* This pyramid is performed by having each of the three players doing a headstand. Each player does a headstand slowly and lifts his legs to the upright position at the same time. The players' feet will be touching each other as they do a headstand.

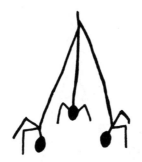

FOUR-AND-FIVE-PERSON PYRAMIDS

1. *The Double Headstand:* This is performed by having three people performing the Flying "W" in the center and two outside players doing headstands on the side.

2. *The Brooklyn Bridge:* This is a combination pyramid that consists of two double-high-kneeling players topped by a standing player.

3. *The Topper Pyramid:* This consists of two kneeling players on the bottom. The third player stands astride of the two players. The fourth player stands on the knees of the third player. The third player holds on to the legs of the top player.

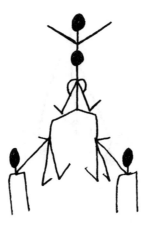

4. *The High-Topper Pyramid:* This is similar to the Topper, except that the two bottom players are standing.

Challenge your students to think up other pyramid formations that they can use that have more than five players in them. Can your class develop a pyramid that uses all of the students and is at least two stories high?

centipede crawl (k-2)

Social Awareness: cooperating in a group
Equipment: none

Procedure: Select several players to start this activity. The first player gets down on her hands and knees while the next player gets on the back of the first player. The second player wraps his legs around the waist of the first player and leans forward until both players can place their hands on the ground. They both begin to walk with four hands and two feet. Let them practice until it becomes easy to perform. Let an additional player get on the back of the lead player and wrap his legs about the lead player's waist. All the players then place their hands on the ground as before. This makes a six-hand–two-feet centipede.

Add other students to the centipede to make it larger.

skin the snake (k-2)

Social Awareness: cooperating with a group
Equipment: none

Procedure: Select two groups of players. They stand in a single file. Each player extends her right hand backwards between her legs. At the same time, the player grasps the hand of the player in front of her with her left hand.

On a signal, the players on each team start moving backwards. The last player in line starts to lie down on the ground while still holding on to the hand of the player in front of him. The next to the last player then straddles the last player who is lying down and lies down too. This continues until all the players are lying down. After all the players are lying down, the last player on the line stands up and walks forward in a straddle position. As this is done, he pulls forward the next player. This action is continued until all the players are back on their feet again.

Remind all the players to keep their grasp tight throughout this game.

wiggle worm (k-2)

Social Awareness: cooperating with a group
Equipment: none

Procedure: Select several students to start this activity. The students sit down in a row. The students form a "Wiggle Worm" by wrapping their legs about the waist of the player in front of them. These players then practice moving by wiggling and using their hands to support their bodies. After this group is able to move without breaking apart, you can add other students to the Wiggle Worm.

mule kick (k-up)

Body Awareness: balancing skills
Equipment: mats

Procedure: This individual skill is attempted by placing the hands on the ground. The player then kicks his feet up in the air while supporting himself with his arms. Encourage the more advanced students to try to kick their feet high in the air. A few students may be able to kick up into a momentary handstand position. This stunt is called a mule kick because it resembles an angry mule as it kicks its hind legs in the air.

tuck jump (k-up)

Body Awareness: jumping skills
Equipment: none

Procedure: This stunt is performed by having the player try to jump high enough to assume a tuck position while in the air. The tuck position should be performed quickly, with the student bringing her knees into her chest and wrapping her arms about her knees. This movement should be rapid enough to allow the performer to land on the ground in a standing position.

seal walk (k-up)

Body Awareness: physical fitness
Equipment: mats

Procedure: This individual stunt is performed by having your students drag themselves across the floor with their arms. The students lie on the floor in a prone position. The legs are outstretched and their bodies are supported by their arms. By moving their arms, the students can drag themselves across the floor in an action resembling the movements of a seal.

three-person walk (2-up)

Social Awareness: cooperating with a group
Equipment: cardboard boxes

Procedure: This is a good group activity. Start by selecting three students. These three players perform a group walk by standing shoulder to shoulder in a line. The middle player's feet are placed in two cardboard boxes, one for each foot. The outside players stick their inside feet into the boxes too. This three-player group then attempts to walk for a certain distance. Once these three players have practiced walking with the boxes, you can add additional players to the group. Each new player takes another cardboard box.

It can get quite tricky with more than three players.

pop up (2-up)

Body Awareness: jumping skills
Equipment: mats

Procedure: This individual stunt is performed by having the student stand on his knees. He then attempts to quickly jump up from his knees to a standing position. This is done by swinging the arms upward as the jump is made.

class fall (3-up)

Body Awareness: upper body fitness and balancing skills
Equipment: none

Procedure: Have each student select a partner. The partners line up facing each other, forming two parallel lines. The two lines should be about two feet away from each other. On a signal, both groups fall toward the center. Each student cushions the fall by placing the palms of her hands against her partner's. As the two partners meet in the center, they will be supporting their weight on their hands to form an A-frame figure.
See how many students can hold this formation for more than ten seconds.

the magic carpet (5-up)

Social Awareness: cooperating in a group
Equipment: mats

Procedure: This group activity is an outstanding one. Select one player to lie down on a mat. This student should be on his back. Eight other students are placed around the edges of this mat. On a signal, these eight players grab the edges of the mat and slowly lift the mat and the student off the ground. The floor area should be covered with mats also.
The mat can be lifted to waist level as the "magic carpet" is taken for a short trip around the immediate area. The mat is then slowly lowered back onto the ground. This continues until every student has had a chance to be on the mat.

INNOVATIVE

AND

Creative Activities

Have you ever wondered how to play Frisbee* golf? How to use scooter boards? How to teach your class the use of parachutes for exciting cooperative games? If you answered "yes" to any of these questions, then this chapter is for you.

Chapter 8 is divided into the following sections:

- Parachute Games
- Frisbee Games for Fun
- Scooter Board Activities and Games
- Games to Play on a Limited Budget

*Frisbee is a trademark of Wham-O Manufacturing Co.

During the past several years, there has been an increasing interest in playing with parachutes. Many companies even manufacture parachutes for school use. Whether you use a real parachute or a specially made one, however, you and your students will have fun with the following activities.

merry-go-round (k-2)

Body Awareness: developing locomotor movements
Equipment: parachute; record player; records

Procedure: This is a listening activity that your students will find fun. Have all your students hold the parachute with the right hand. They walk around the parachute in a clockwise direction. On a signal, the class turns and walks in the opposite direction. Other locomotor skills can be used while the students are using the parachute, such as galloping, sliding, grapevine steps, skipping, and other movements. Play music to add to the enjoyment.

row boat (k-2)

Body Awareness: physical fitness
Equipment: parachute

Procedure: Have your students sit around the edges of the parachute. The students sit with their legs extended under the parachute as they hold on to the edges of the parachute. The students bend forward and touch their toes. They move their arms backwards in a rowing motion. The parachute should be pulled taut. Repeat this exercise for several minutes.

leg march (k-2)

Body Awareness: physical fitness
Equipment: parachute

Procedure: The students sit under the edges of the parachute. They hold the parachute with their hands. They move forward by keeping their legs extended and their feet pointed toward the center. The students scoot forward and then back. As the students move backwards, they pull the edges of the parachute until it is taut.

making waves (k-up)

Body Awareness: physical fitness
Equipment: parachute

Procedure: Have your class scattered around the edge of the parachute. Each student holds on to the parachute's perimeter with both hands. The students lift the parachute up to waist level and make waves by quickly shaking the parachute. This causes the parachute to ripple and resemble waves of the ocean.

making a dome (k-up)

Body Awareness: physical fitness
Equipment: parachute

Procedure: Your class can make a parachute dome by lifting the parachute up above their heads. The students lift the parachute high above their heads and take three steps toward the center. This causes the parachute to rise in a domelike mushroom shape.

jaws (k-up)

Body Awareness: physical fitness
Equipment: parachute

Procedure: The students are scattered around the edge of the parachute. The parachute is held about waist high and shaken gently. Select one player to be the Shark. The Shark goes under the parachute and "swims" around. She holds her hands near her head so that this resembles the fin of a shark. The object of the game is to grab another player's leg. This player then screams and takes the place of the Shark. The Shark takes the place of this student. The game continues with this player grabbing the leg of another student.

Play until all your students have had a chance to be the Shark.

number exchange (2-up)

Body Awareness: physical fitness
Equipment: parachute

Procedure: The students are scattered around the edge of the parachute. The class is divided into two groups and each member in each group is given a number. For example, if there are twenty-six students in your class, you will have one half of the class number off from 1 to 13, and the other half numbers off from 1 to 13 again. This should result in the players with the same numbers opposite each other. The teacher then calls a certain number. The players with this number have to run under the parachute and exchange positions. The rest of the class lifts the parachute as the number is called. Give every player the opportunity to run under the parachute as it is lifted. Remind your students not to bring the parachute down too quickly, as this might cause the running players to get hurt.

popcorn (2-up)

Body Awareness: physical fitness
Equipment: parachute; several beanbags

Procedure: Place the beanbags in the center of the parachute. The class tries to shake the beanbags out of the parachute. This resembles a huge popcorn machine as the beanbags "pop" high into the air. Assign several players to be the popcorn collectors. They gather up the beanbags and throw them back into the parachute.

parachute ball (2-up)

Body Awareness: physical fitness
Equipment: parachute; one utility ball

Procedure: Your students are scattered around the edge of the parachute. The class is divided into two groups that occupy both halves of the parachute circle. A playground ball is placed in the center of the parachute. The object of the game is to shake the ball off on the opponent's side of the parachute. This scores one point. The first team to score three points is the winner.

parachute race (2-up)

Social Awareness: cooperating with a group
Equipment: two parachutes; two traffic cones

Procedure: Divide your class into two teams. Each team is given a parachute to work with. The two parachutes are centered over each of the traffic cones that are placed about fifty feet apart from each other. On a signal, the players of each parachute try to center their parachute on their opponent's traffic cone. This is an interesting race that requires that all the members to cooperate and run as a single unit. The first team to center their parachute over the traffic cone is the winner.

hole in one (2-up)

Body Awareness: physical fitness
Equipment: parachute; four tennis balls; felt-tipped pen

Procedure: The students are scattered around the edge of the parachute. Divide the class into two teams. Four tennis balls are placed in the parachute. Mark two of the balls so that there are two balls marked and two unmarked. Each group tries to shake one of its balls into the small hole in the center of the parachute.

Award one point for each ball that goes into the center.

Interest in "flying disc" sports has rapidly increased over the past few years, with many youngsters finding that the Frisbee offers an exciting array of game possibilities. Several of these interesting activities are described here.

frisbee fun toss (k-up)

Body Awareness: catching and throwing skills
Equipment: one Frisbee per group

Procedure: Divide the rest of your class into small groups of four to six players. The members of each group stand side by side in a row. One player in each group is selected to be the first Leader. The Leader stands in front of her group at a distance of twelve to fifteen feet away. The Leader throws the Frisbee to each of the players in her group. The players return the Frisbee to the leader in turn.

197

This activity is one that encourages your students to develop the throwing and catching skills needed for the other Frisbee activities. Once the entire group has been given a chance to throw the Frisbee, the Leader goes to the end of the line, and the next player becomes the Leader.

Your older students will enjoy the addition of one or more of the following modifications:

1. If a player misses the Frisbee, that player has to go to the end of the line. If the Leader misses the disc, he has to go to the end of the line, and the next player takes his place.

2. The distance between the players and the Leader can be increased.

3. Encourage your students to try to catch the Frisbee with one hand. You may designate that all players have to catch with their left hand only.

4. Have the first player in the line run to a certain point to receive the Frisbee from the Leader. This gives your students practice in catching and throwing the disc to a moving player.

frisbee golf (2-up)

Body Awareness: throwing skills
Equipment: one Frisbee per student; "golf" course

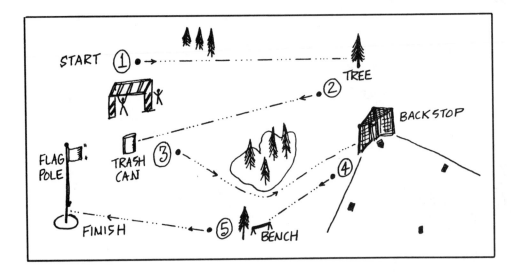

Procedure: This game is played like a regular game of golf, except that a Frisbee is used in place of a golf ball. The students are either paired up one against another or in small teams of two or more players. The object of the game is to "hole out" in as few throws as possible. Each player starts from the tee area and has to throw the Frisbee toward a tree or other object that is designated as the hole.

If you are playing as small teams, each player rotates the throws in order. The Frisbee must hit the tree or other object to successfully count. You can design a small Frisbee golf course such as the one shown or let your students make up their own.

keep away (3-up)

Body Awareness: catching and throwing skills
Equipment: one Frisbee

Procedure: This activity is a great lead-up activity for Frisbee football. The object of the activity is to keep the Frisbee from a group of opponents. Divide your class into various teams of six to eight players. Two teams play against each other on a grassy area. The Frisbee is given to one of the teams. On a signal, the Frisbee is passed from player to player. The players on the opposite team try to intercept the disc. There is no scoring in this teaching activity. The goal of each team is to see if they can keep the Frisbee from their opponents.

Do not allow any player contact that would cause possible injury. Tripping, pushing, kicking, and other fouls are not permitted.

falling stars (3-up)

Body Awareness: catching and throwing skills
Equipment: one Frisbee

Procedure: Divide your class into groups of six to eight players. Have two teams play against each other on a soft surface area. The players on each team are numbered in order. The first player on one team is given the Frisbee. This player throws the disc high into the air. All the members on the other team try to catch the disc. If the disc is caught, one point is scored for that team. The number 1 player on this team then throws the Frisbee back to the starting team. The throw is once again a high one. This continues with each team alternating throws.

Award one point for each successful catch a team makes.

Play several rounds. The team with the most points at the end of the game will be the winner.

gym frisbee (3-up)

Body Awareness: throwing and running skills
Equipment: one Frisbee; two bases; two traffic cones

Procedure: This activity is played inside a gym or on a rectangular playing area outside. An outdoor basketball court makes an excellent playing area. Set up the two bases and the markers for the restraining line as shown.

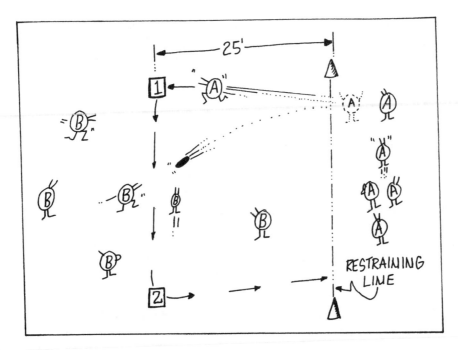

Select eight to twelve players on each team. The object of the game is for team members to throw the Frisbee into the playing area from any place behind the restraining line. The Frisbee needs to be thrown between the two sidelines onto the playing court. Once a player does this, he will run to first base. The outfield team retrieves the disc and tries to get the runner out in the following ways:

1. The runner is out if he is hit/tagged by the disc while running to a base.
2. The runner is out if he is not on a base when the Frisbee is thrown back over the restraining line by the outfield team.

Each runner tries to run to first base before the disc is thrown back over the restraining line or is hit by the disc. The runners progress from first base to second base and then to across the restraining line at any point. There can be any number of runners on a base at a time.

Any runner who is not on a base when the Frisbee is thrown over the restraining line is called out. Once a player is out, he is no longer able to play for that inning. When all the players on the throwing team are out, or when there are no players left to throw the Frisbee because all the players are on base, the outfield team gets to line up behind the restraining line as the two teams change sides.

Score one point each time a player gets back across the restraining line. The fielding team can also score points by catching the Frisbee on a fly. One point is awarded to the outfield team for this. The runner is *not called out* if his disc is caught. He will run the bases as would any other player who has thrown the Frisbee into fair territory.

The team with the most points at the end of the playing time is the winner.

frisbee football (4-up)

Body Awareness: throwing and catching skills
Equipment: one Frisbee

Procedure: This activity is played on a football field area. There are two goal lines on opposite ends of the field. The object of this game is to throw the Frisbee into your own end zone so that it is grabbed by one of your players. If the Frisbee is caught in the end zone before touching the ground, the team scores six points. If the Frisbee touches the ground and the Frisbee is retrieved by a team member, then the team scores only three points. Frisbees that are retrieved by the other team score no points.

The play in this activity is simple. The flying disc is thrown from player to player down the field. Members on the opposite team try to intercept the disc. Players are not allowed to touch one another during the game. Players with the Frisbee cannot run with the disc. They can only pass the disc to other players. Opponents are not allowed to grab the Frisbee from an opponent.

Any infractions reward the opposite team with a free throw-in from the point of the infraction.

Start the game by having both groups lined up about fifty feet apart from each other. Select one team to throw the Frisbee to its opponents.

Play for four ten-minute quarters.

Scooter boards can provide hours of fun and excitement for your students. Like parachute games, scooter board activities have been found to be instant student pleasers.

musical leader (k-2)

Body Awareness: moving to various rhythms
Equipment: one scooter board per couple; record player; records

Procedure: Select couples so that one player is on the scooter board and the other player is pushing. One player is selected to be the Musical Leader. The Musical Leader picks a certain spot on the playing surface. This spot will be the "magic spot."

As the music begins, all the couples move about the area. The pushers should try to move the scooter boards to the rhythm of the music. When the music stops, all the players freeze. The player sitting on the scooter board that is closest to the "magic spot" is the next Musical Leader. The old Musical Leader becomes the new pusher of that couple. The old pusher sits on the scooter board, as the music continues.

Play this game for as long as you like. Use different moods and rhythms of music for your students to enjoy. Have the couples change places after every round so that they all have a chance to push and sit on the board.

buggy-ride relay (k-3)

Body Awareness: physical fitness
Equipment: four scooter boards

Procedure: Divide your class into four smaller groups. This relay activity is similar to the chariot relay. The first player sits on the scooter board. The second player grabs onto the spread legs of the first player. On a signal, the player holding onto the legs of the seated player starts to run to the turning line and back.

The rider then goes to the end of the line. The runner sits on the scooter board as the next player becomes the new runner.

The first group to finish is the winner.

backward relay (k-up)

Body Awareness: physical fitness and developing leg muscles
Equipment: four scooter boards

Procedure: Divide your class into four smaller groups. The object of this relay is to move the scooter board to a designated turning line and back. This is done by having the student sit on the scooter board, facing toward the back. The student pushes the board forward by pushing off with her legs.

Since your students will be moving backward, encourage them to watch out for other players.

speedway relay (k-up)

Body Awareness: physical fitness
Equipment: four scooter boards

Procedure: Divide your class into four groups. The object of this relay is to propel the scooter board from the starting line, around a designated turning line, and back again. This is done by grasping the board with two hands and pushing the board as the student runs. Your students will find that they can go quite fast in this manner.

knee-sit relay (2-up)

Body Awareness: physical fitness and developing upper body strength
Equipment: four scooter boards

Procedure: Divide your class into four smaller groups. In this relay, your students kneel on the board and move themselves with their arms. This is an excellent way to develop upper body strength and have fun at the same time.

partner-push relay (2-up)

Body Awareness: physical fitness
Equipment: four scooter boards

Procedure: Divide your class into four groups. This relay uses two players on each team at a time. The first player in each group sits on the scooter board. The second player then pushes the first player to the designated turning line and back. When they are back at their group, the first player goes to the end of the line while the pushing player sits on the board. The next player becomes the new pusher.

   The first team to finish is declared the winner.

chariot relay (2-up)

Body Awareness: physical fitness
Equipment: four scooter boards; four ropes

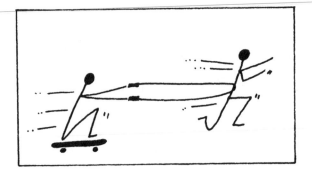

Procedure: This exciting relay is the best of the best. Divide your class into four groups. The first two players on each team act as a pair. The first player sits on the scooter board. The second player becomes the Horse and pulls the scooter board and the Rider. The rope is placed about the waist of the Horse, and each end is grabbed by the Rider. On a signal, the "chariots" take off to circle a designated turning point and back. The Rider then goes to the back of his line, while the Horse becomes the new Rider. The next player in line becomes the new Horse.

   This relay continues until all the players have had a chance to be the Rider and Horse. Declare the first group to finish the winners.

shooting gallery (2-up)

Body Awareness: dodging and throwing skills
Equipment: two scooter boards; several foam-rubber balls

Procedure: Divide your class into two groups. The players of one group make two parallel lines. The two lines should be about 20 feet apart and facing each other. On a signal, a player on the other team grasps the scooter board in her hands and tries to move between the two lines without being hit by the foam-rubber balls.

The players in the lines throw the foam-rubber balls at the scooter board Runner. If the Runner is hit, a second Runner with a scooter board can start to run. Score one point for every player who gets through the double line without being hit by the foam-rubber ball. When all the players have had a chance to run, change sides.

Play this game for several rotations and award the team with the most points the title of "Stupendous Scooter Scramblers!"

dry land swimmers' relay (3-up)

Body Awareness: physical fitness and developing upper body strength
Equipment: four scooter boards

Procedure: Divide your class into four groups. Each group lines up in a single file. The object of this wonderful fitness relay is to move the scooter board around a designated turning line and back to the starting point. The students lie on the scooter board and have the board situated at about the hips area. The students use their arms to pull themselves forward. This action resembles a swimmer practicing the freestyle stroke.

The first group to finish is declared the winner.

scooter-board polo (3-up)

Body Awareness: throwing and catching skills
Equipment: five scooter boards; four traffic cones; one soccer ball

Procedure: This activity resembles a water polo match. The play can take place on a gym floor or outside on a basketball court. Select ten players to be divided into two teams. Set up two goals, one on either end of the court.

The object of the game is for one team to pass the ball from player to player and into a ten-foot-wide goal. Each player must sit on the scooter board. He cannot kneel or stand on the board, but must remain in the sitting position throughout the game.

Each team has one Goalie who situates himself near the goal. If a ball passes between the two goal markers, one point is scored.

The game is started with one team given the ball out of bounds. Once a player is in control of the ball, he cannot be touched by an opponent. This player tries to pass the ball to another player on his team. Once a player has the ball, he can be allowed two gliding pushes. That is, he can push his scooter board and glide along the floor two times before he has to stop and pass the ball. The opponents can try to get the ball away from the player, but cannot touch the player with the ball. As in the game of basketball, an opponent can try to knock the ball away. If he touches any part of the player in the process, the ball is taken out of bounds by the team that originally had the ball.

Tripping, slapping, or hitting is not allowed.

Play four quarters of ten minutes each. The team that scores the most goals is declared the winner. You can rotate other players into the game by changing all the players after a goal is made.

scooter boppers (3-up)

Body Awareness: throwing, catching, and dodging skills
Equipment: four or more scooter boards; several foam-rubber balls

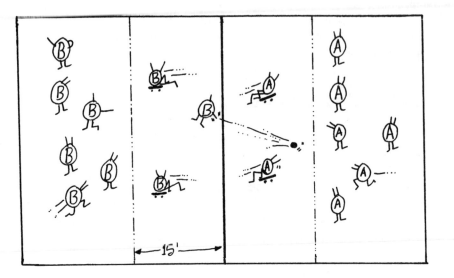

Procedure: Select two groups. Each group takes its place on one side of the playing court. A basketball court area can be used if you want to play outdoors. Each team has two or more players who will sit on the scooter boards. These players try to dodge the balls as they are thrown. The scooter board players can move only in their respective areas as indicated in the diagram. The object of the game is to hit one of the opponents on the scooter board. When this takes place, the player on the board must change places with the player who hit her. All the other players who are not on the scooter boards must stay behind the restraining lines to catch a loose ball. Once a ball is retrieved, the player is allowed to cross the restraining line and move as close to the center line as possible. The throws must take place behind the center line.

The players on the scooter boards are not allowed to throw the foam-rubber balls.

You can periodically change the players on the scooter boards to ensure that all your students get the chance to be in the center.

blindfold obstacle course (3-up)

Body Awareness: working with an imposed visual loss
Equipment: several scooter boards; several blindfolds; traffic cones

Procedure: Set up a short obstacle course arranging the cones in a zigzag formation. The students in your class are paired up so that one player sits on the scooter board. The other student has the blindfold on. This player will also be the pusher of the player on the scooter board. The object of this activity is for each couple to get through the obstacle course without hitting the markers. The player on the scooter board directs the actions of the pusher.

The directions can be given in several ways:

1. The seated player can tell the pusher how to move.
2. The seated player can "steer" the pushing player by applying pressure to either the pushing player's left or right hand.
3. The seated player can communicate with the pusher with command words. Only the words of "front," "left," "right," "back," and "stop" can be used.

Once all the seated players have finished, have the students change places so that all the players have a chance to experience each role.

scooter-board football (4-up)

Body Awareness: throwing and catching skills
Equipment: twelve scooter boards; one football

Procedure: Select six players to be on each team. The two teams play a game of tag football using the scooters. The players are not allowed to stand or kneel on their boards. They must remain seated at all times.

The play takes place either in the gym or on a basketball court outside.

One team is given the ball to throw to the opposite team. The opposite team retrieves the football and tries to score a touchdown.

This game follows all the rules of tag football. It is a marvelous rainy day activity.

This section will help you to organize and plan an effective elementary physical education program within the means of a limited budget. Described here are plenty of wonderful ways to recycle common items to develop a workable elementary "surplus store" of equipment.

inside, outside, upside down! (k-1)

Cognitive Awareness: exploring spatial words and their meanings
Equipment: three hula hoops of different colors for each group; masking tape

208

Procedure: Tape the three differently colored hoops together as shown.

This hoop triangle is used to challenge your students. Divide your students into groups of six to eight players. Each group has a hoop triangle in front of it. One player in each group responds to certain challenges for a set amount of time. Rotate the students so that every player gets a chance to participate.

Here is a sample of various challenges you can use. The spatial concepts are underlined.

Go <u>through</u> the blue hoop and <u>out</u> the red hoop.

Go <u>in</u> the green hoop leading with one body part and <u>out</u> the blue hoop leading with a different body part.

Hold the blue hoop <u>over</u> your head and then go <u>through</u> each of the three hoops leading with a different body part in each case.

Jump <u>over</u> the red hoop and then jump <u>through</u> another hoop to get <u>out</u>.

Make up other spatial commands as the activity continues.

streamline plastic scoopers (k-2)

Body Awareness: catching and throwing skills
Equipment: several 1-gallon plastic milk containers; scissors; spray paints of various colors

Procedure: Take the plastic milk jugs and cut them as shown.

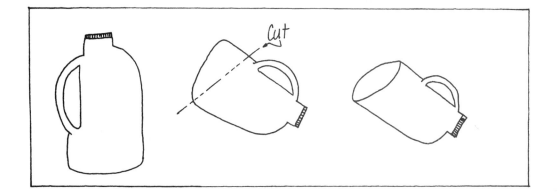

You can color these scoops with spray paint. I have used the three primary colors of red, yellow, and blue to explain to the children the blending of these colors to create other secondary colors. Since the plastic jugs are translucent, the students are able to "mix" the primary colors by placing one jug next to a different colored one.

Let the scoops dry for several hours. After the scoops are dry, you can let your students practice catching and throwing a small ball with their scoops. The students hold the scoop in one hand. A ball is placed inside the scoop. The object of the activity is to catch and throw the ball using different movement patterns. Here are a few challenges that your students will enjoy:

1. Can you throw the ball up in the air and catch it? Can you do this five times in a row without making a mistake? Try it with your other hand. Which way is easier for you?

2. Can you throw the ball up in the air and catch the ball at different levels? Who can throw the ball up high and catch the ball at a low level? Who can catch the ball while on their knees? Lying down? Who can catch the ball at a high level? Who can catch the ball while jumping high in the air?

3. Can you catch the ball while moving in different ways? Who can catch the ball while walking? Skipping? Running? Who can throw the ball against the wall and catch it? Who can walk and let the ball drop on the floor and then catch it?

4. Who can play with a partner? Who can throw the ball to their partner? Can you and your partner throw the ball to each other so that both of you can catch a ball? Explore catching the ball at different levels.

5. Who can try these different stunts? Try to throw the ball up under a leg and then catch the ball. Who can throw the ball up in the air and turn around and catch the ball? Who can throw the ball up, touch their shoulders, and then catch the ball? Try touching your shoulders and knees before catching the ball. Who can throw the ball up and then catch it by putting the scoop under a leg?

Have your students think up other stunts with the scoops.

homemade rainbow balls (k-2)

Body Awareness: catching and throwing skills
Equipment: newspaper; plastic wrap; masking tape; spray paint

Procedure: This is a great way to "mass produce" several dozen small balls at a fast clip. Take the newspaper and crumple it into a small ball.

Use the plastic bread wrapper to cover the ball. Place the newspaper ball in the wrapper. Then tightly wrap the ball with the wrapper.

Use the masking tape and wrap the ball with it. Make sure the ball is tightly wrapped with the tape. Then spray the ball with a bright rainbow design. Use markers to highlight the balls if needed.

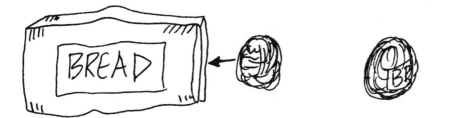

These balls can then be used to practice throwing and catching skills. Challenge your students with the following skills:

1. Try to throw the ball up and clap your hands together. How many times can you clap and still catch the ball? Can you throw the ball up and catch it in the same hand you threw it with? How about throwing the ball from hand to hand?

2. Find a partner. Try rolling the ball to your partner. How about throwing the ball to your partner? Think of other ways to throw the ball to your partner.

hula hoop fractions (k-2)

Cognitive Awareness: math concepts of sets and fractions
Equipment: one hula hoop for every two students; record player; records

Procedure: Arrange the hoops in a scattered formation on the ground. Have each hoop about ten feet away from the other. On a command, your students skip about the hoops going in and out of the hoops. This all takes place as the music plays. When the music stops, the teacher asks the students to get into the hoops in certain sets of players. For example: "All students get in sets of two." All the players then try to get in sets of two and stand in the center of one hoop. This continues as the music is restarted, and another command is given when the music is stopped. Have your students get in various different sets.

All players get in sets of four.

All players get in sets of six.

All players get in sets of three.

You will find that many students will be unable to get in certain sets. Encourage these students to quickly find a hula hoop anyway. You can then ask these students how many more players they would need to complete their set.

You can also practice the concept of fractions using the hoops. When your students are in a certain set, ask one player in each group to step outside the hoop. For example, if all the students were in sets of three, you could explore the fractions that make up "thirds." Ask one player to step outside the hoop. You would then have *one third of the set outside* the hoop and *two thirds of the set in* the hoop. This can be repeated with other fractions. Your students will begin to understand the use and concept of sixths, eighths, and other simple fractions in this manner.

beanbag helpers (k-2)

Body Awareness: balancing skills
Equipment: beanbags; record player; records

Procedure: Each player will decide what body part to balance her beanbag on. Some players may balance the beanbag on their heads or shoulders or feet. The music plays as the players move about the room to the music. When a beanbag falls off a student, that student must freeze. Other players then try to pick the beanbag up off the ground and place it back on the player's body. This has to be done very carefully so that their beanbag does not fall off.

Play this game for several rounds. On each round, play a different type of music—a classic waltz, a jazz piece, or a modern disco tuńe.

Have your students explore which types of music made their balancing easier and what pieces made balancing harder. Can rhythm dictate certain movements and actions?

After the activity is over you can further explore the role of a helper in various games and activities.

the wiggle-worm rope (k-2)

Body Awareness: jumping and landing skills
Equipment: one long jump rope; mats

Procedure: This activity will help your students to gain jumping skills and learn to land correctly. Place two or more gymnastics mats on the ground. Two students are selected to be the Helpers. The Helpers hold the ends of the long jump rope. The two Helpers should be standing beside the mats. The mats are between the rope holders and help cushion the jumps of the students.

One by one, the students run and jump over the rope. The rope should be held about one foot off the ground. Encourage the students to land with their legs bent. They should "give" with their legs as they land.

The two helpers raise the rope after each round.

balloon explorers (k-2)

Body Awareness: developing eye-hand coordination and striking skills
Equipment: one balloon per student

Procedure: Give a balloon to each student. Each student can blow the balloon up. Have all the students line up on one side of the playing area. The object of this activity is for the students to explore the different ways they can use the balloon. Challenge them with the following:

1. Move the balloon from one side of the playing area to the other side by striking it with your hands . . . with your head . . . with your feet . . . with your left hand and right foot. Explore using different body parts with which to strike the balloon.

2. Partner skills—can you and your partner move the balloon to the other side using hands only? Feet? One foot and one hand?

Can you and your partner hold the balloon between your backs and walk to the other side of the playing area? Between your heads? Your shoulders?

Can you volley the balloon between you and your partner? How long can you and your partner keep the balloon up?

scoop and catch (k-2)

Body Awareness: developing eye-hand coordination
Equipment: several 1-gallon plastic milk containers; string; several wooden thread spools

Procedure: You can make a great indoor eye-hand coordination skill game by recycling a few household items.
Here's how to do it:

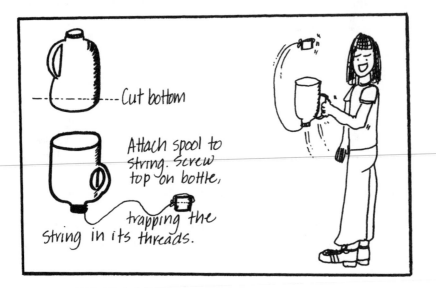

beanbag challenges (k-3)

Body Awareness: balancing, catching and throwing skills, and identifying body parts
Equipment: one beanbag per student

Procedure: Each student is given a beanbag. Have your students explore the following skills and challenges:

1. Catching and throwing the beanbag.

   "Who can throw the beanbag up in the air and catch it?"
   "Can you catch the beanbag after clapping your hands two times?"
   "Can you turn around and catch the beanbag?"
   "Can you toss the beanbag from hand to hand?"

2. Catching and throwing while moving.

   "Who can catch the beanbag while walking?"
   "Can you walk backwards and catch the beanbag?"
   "How about skipping?" "Hopping?" "Running?"

3. Catching and throwing in different directions.

"Throw the beanbag in front of you and catch it."

"Can you throw the beanbag behind you and catch it?"

"Sideways?"

4. Balancing the beanbag on different body parts.

"Can you balance the beanbag on your head and walk?"

"Can you place the beanbag on your shoulder and balance on one foot?"

"Can you balance the beanbag on your left knee and hop?"

You can encourage the students to explore other stunts they can do with the beanbag.

homemade hula hoops (k-up)

Body Awareness: gross motor coordination

Equipment: black plastic water piping (available at hardward stores); wooden dowels; nails; hammer; saw (to be used only under teacher supervision); colored fabric tape

Procedure: What a great way to make your own hula hoops!

Just cut the piping into suitable lengths. Seven- to eight-foot lengths are recommended. Since the piping may vary in density, you can experiment in finding a length that will easily bend. Take a small piece of dowel and use the nails or staples to ;ecure the ends of the hoop together.

You can use different colored fabric tape to cover the connected ends. This will add ↄ little color to the hoop. You may also use the tape to create a stripe on the hoop by curling the tape about the hoop in a spiral.

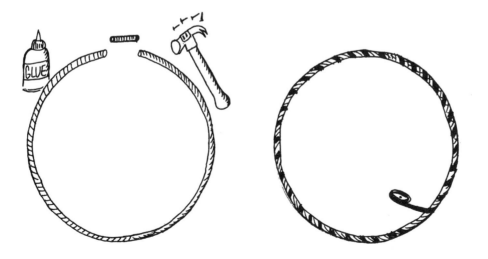

Challenge your students to explore all the different ways they can use the hoops. The following activities are some that you and your students may enjoy.

hula-hoop throw (k-up)

Body Awareness: accurate throwing skills
Equipment: one hula hoop for every four students; three small balls for every four students

Procedure: Divide your class into groups of four. One person rolls the hoop while the other three players try to throw their ball into the rolling target. Score one point for each ball thrown in the hoop. Play several rounds with the players rotating positions. The player with the most points at the end of the activity is the winner. Actually, all your students will be winners. Each one will have enjoyed the activity and gained valuable accuracy throwing skills.

easy-to-make beanbags (k-up)

Body Awareness: catching and throwing skills
Equipment: pieces of cloth; dried beans; sewing machine or needle and thread; scissors

Procedure: Cut the cloth into a five-inch square. The cloth should be folded as shown. The cloth should be folded with the design side on the inside of the square.

Sew two edges of the square together, leaving the third edge open. Then pull the square through the opening so that the design side is showing. Fill the bag with beans. Sew the bag together.

Beanbags can be used to introduce your students to many catching and throwing activities. The beanbags are easier to catch than a ball, and the beanbags can be balanced on different body parts to increase your students' body awareness.

jump ropes (k-up)

Body Awareness: developing eye-hand and eye-foot coordination and physical fitness skills

Equipment: heavy-duty rope of ½" diameter; rope knife; colored fabric tape

Procedure: Take the rope and cut it into lengths to suit your students. The ropes can be measured by having a student hold the rope as shown. The rope should reach the top of the student's shoulders. Tape the ends of the rope with colored fabric tape. You may want to use different colored tape to mark the lengths of the ropes. For example:

Short ropes (six feet) can be red.

Medium ropes (seven feet) can be blue.

Long ropes (eight feet) can be yellow.

Longer ropes (sixteen to twenty feet) can be green. These longer ropes can be used by your students in group long-rope activities.

You and your students can explore jumping the rope in individual and group sessions.

stretch loops (k-up)

Body Awareness: physical fitness
Equipment: inner tubes or rubber surgical tubing; scissors

Procedure: Stretch loops are fantastic items to have whenever you are trying to incorporate a physical fitness unit with your physical education program. The stretch loops can be used to develop certain large body muscles as your students stretch and bend to music.

   Here are the two different ways to make them:

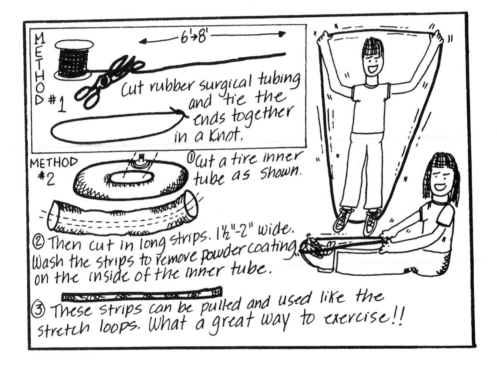

   Now that your stretch loops are made, you can use a few of the following exercise suggestions.

stretch-loop activities (k-up)

Body Awareness: physical fitness
Equipment: stretch loops; record player; records

Procedure: Each student is given a stretch loop. Select a record that has a good beat to it. Have your students follow you as they exercise to the music in the following ways:

   1. Hold the loop in each hand. In rhythm to the music, have the students pull the loop in an outward direction. This develops upper body strength. This exercise can be

done at different sides of the body and at different levels. For example, you could start the exercise at chest height for four beats. You could then continue this four-beat pull at several different places—overhead, to the left side, to the middle, to the right side.

2. Have the students hold the loop in each hand. Have them stand on the middle of the loop and pull the loop upwards from side to side, alternating arms . . . with both arms . . . with one arm at a time.

3. Have the students sit down on the ground and stretch the loop around their feet with outstretched legs. They pull the loop in a rowing motion to the music. In the same manner, they flex and extend their legs to the music.

You could also have a few students make up a routine to exercise with a certain record.

Feel free to add other aerobic exercises to the loop exercises. It is a good idea to use both types of exercises when moving to the music.

carpet squares (k-up)

Body Awareness: physical fitness
Equipment: carpet square samples from retail carpet centers

Procedure: You can use these carpet squares as you would scooter boards. The carpet squares are turned upside down so that the fibers are facing the gym floor. This allows the carpet to skim over the floor. Divide your class into smaller groups. Use the carpet squares with these suggested activities:

1. Have your students place their hands on the carpet square. On a signal, the students push the carpet square to a designated turning point and back.

2. One student sits on the carpet square. The next player pushes him to the wall and back. The seated player goes to the end of the line as the pushing player sits on the carpet square. The next player becomes the new pusher.

3. Horse and wagon relay—the first player sits on the carpet square. The player behind her grabs onto this player's outstretched legs. The object is for the pair to move from the starting line and back again. The Horse pulls the Rider along the gym floor. The Rider goes to the end of the line. The Horse becomes the new Rider as the next player becomes the new Horse.

You can also use the other activities that are found in the scooter board section for carpet square ideas.

hula-hoop relay (2-up)

Body Awareness: gross motor coordination
Equipment: four hula hoops; several basketballs

Procedure: Select four different teams. The object of the relay is to have the first player move to the designated turning point and back. While the players move to the turning point, they must keep the hula hoop rotating about their hips. This makes the relay quite interesting. The players cannot walk too fast or else they will lose control of their hoops.

You may repeat this relay by having the players use different body parts to rotate the hoop about. Add another facet to this relay by having the students dribble a ball as they move with the hoop.

jumping activities (2-up)

Body Awareness: physical fitness and coordination
Equipment: jump ropes

Procedure: Listed below are suggested rope activities that you can use with your students.

INDIVIDUAL ROPE JUMPING
1. Stand on one foot. Hop on this foot and let the rope pass under it.
2. Stand on both feet. Hop with both feet and let the rope pass under them.
3. Start with one foot in front of the other. Jump with one foot and then the other. Continue alternating feet.
4. Skip backwards using the skills described above.
5. Jump in place and cross the legs back and forth from a straddle position to a crossed position.

LONG-ROPE JUMPING
1. Enter the swinging rope and exit on the other side.
2. Enter the swinging rope, take one jump, and come out the other side.
3. Enter the swinging rope, take one jump turning one-half turn, and jump out backwards.
4. Enter the swinging rope, take a few jumps, and exit from the same side.

stomp board (2-up)

Body Awareness: catching skills
Equipment: pieces of 2" x 4" pine; saw (to be used only under teacher supervision); nails; hammer; beanbags; spray paint

Procedure: A stomp board is used to practice catching skills. You can make a quick and easy stomp board as shown.

Place a beanbag on the tip of the stomp board. Stomp down on the other end of the board with your heel. The beanbag will fly up in the air. The object of the activity is to try to catch the beanbag. Your older students will like the challenge of trying to catch more than one beanbag. Place the beanbags side by side on the end of the board. If the bags are placed one on top of the other, the beanbags will not fly high enough for your students to catch.

Try two beanbags at first. If your students can easily catch two at a time, encourage them to try three.

crazy hoop ball (3-up)

Body Awareness: pitching, hitting, running, and moving skills
Equipment: softball field; hula hoop; one tennis ball; one tennis racket; four bases

Procedure: This game is played on a softball field. Select two teams of eight to fifteen players. One team is in the outfield in a scattered formation. The other team lines up near home plate. A hula hoop lies in the field about fifty feet from home plate. A pitcher pitches the tennis ball to the first player. The player tries to hit the ball with the tennis racquet. The object of the game is for the batter to hit the ball with the racquet as far as possible. The batter then starts to run the bases. The outfield team retrieves the ball as quickly as possible. When the ball is retrieved it is passed from one player to another toward the hula hoop. The ball must be passed to the Hoop Holder, a player on the outfield team who was selected beforehand. Once the Hoop Holder has the ball, he will hold the hoop up so that all the players on his team can run through the hoop. When the last player passes through the hoop, all the players on his team shout "Hoopball!"

This stops the runner from running the bases. If the outfield team shouts "Hoopball!" before the batter gets back to home plate, the batter is out. If not, the batting team scores one point. The batter is also out if the ball is caught in the air. After three outs, the teams exchange sides. You may also want to make the distance between bases farther if it seems to be too easy for the batters to score.

Play for several innings. The team with the most points is the winner.

hurdles (3-up)

Body Awareness: tracking skills
Equipment: traffic cones and jump ropes *or* plastic bottles and string

Procedure: Use the traffic cones and ropes (empty plastic bottles and string) to make hurdles for your students.

You can make the hurdles as shown.

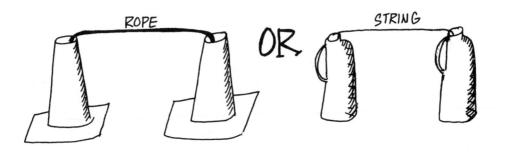

Set up three or more of the hurdles for your track stars to practice their quick-stepping running skills. You can also use two sets of hurdles to have interclass races.

beanbag egg toss (3-up)

Body Awareness: throwing and catching skills
Equipment: one beanbag for every two students

Procedure: Have your students form in pairs. Each pair should line up in two lines. These two lines should be about five feet away from each other. Each of the players should be facing her partner. On a signal, all the students toss the beanbag to their partners. If the beanbag is caught, the players can take a small step backward. If the beanbag is dropped, the players stay where they are.

Each time a successful catch is performed, the two players can take a small step backward. Encourage your students to concentrate on making accurate throws to their partners.

Also remind the students to throw the beanbags only upon your signal. You'll have more control over the group if everyone throws the beanbag at the same time.

wooden stilts (3-up)

Body Awareness: coordinating movements and balancing skills
Equipment: long pieces of 2″ x 4″ pine; saw (to be used only under teacher supervision); nails; hammer

Procedure: How about making a pair of wooden stilts? Use the diagram to show how to build a pair or two for your students.

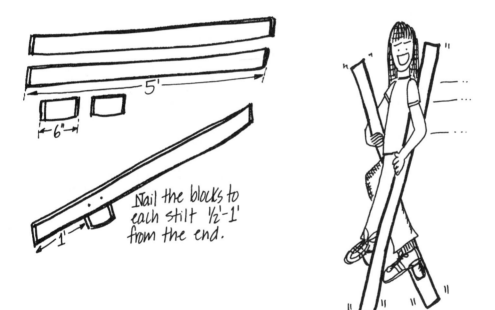

Nail the blocks to each stilt ½'-1' from the end.

You might like to have an interesting wooden stilts relay race once all your students learn to walk with the stilts.

milk-jug fencing (3-up)

Body Awareness: developing eye-hand coordination and balancing skills
Equipment: one 1-gallon plastic milk container per student

Procedure: Have your students select a partner to play with. Each student is given a milk jug. They hold the jug upside down by the handle. This makes a suitable and safe fencing foil. Each player stands on a designated line. The object of the game is to knock the other player off the line. Once the two players have started, they cannot move their feet.

free-for-all! (4-up)

Body Awareness: running and agility skills
Equipment: one balloon per student; string

Procedure: Have all your students blow up the balloon and tie it to one of their feet with a piece of string. The string should be long enough so that the balloon dangles from the student's foot.

   The object of the activity is for each student to try to step on the balloon of other students while keeping his balloon protected. Once a student's balloon is popped, that student sits down. Only the players with balloons are allowed to continue in the activity.

   Continue playing until there is only one student left.